Grades 1–3

Problem Play

Stephen Currie

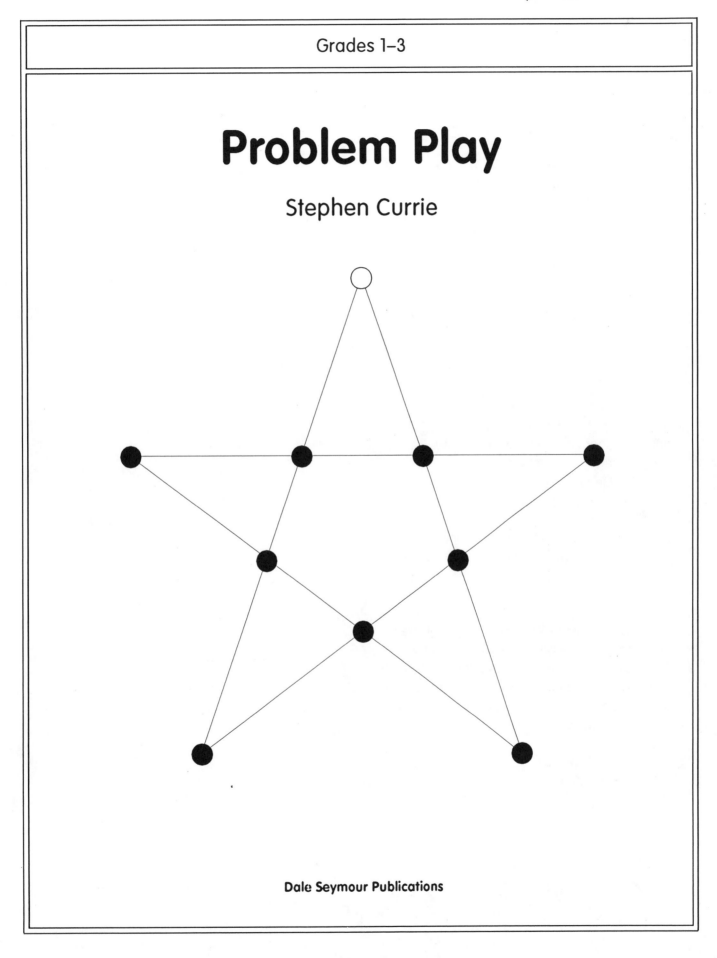

Dale Seymour Publications

Acknowledgements

Many children and teachers have played a role in making this book what it is. I would particularly like to thank Mary Ellen Kenny, Harriet Finkelstein, and, of course, my wife Amity.

Managing Editor: Mike Kane
Project Editor: Joan Gideon
Production Coordinator: Karen Edmonds
Design Manager: Jeff Kelly
Art: Rachel Gage
Cover Artist: Terry Toyama

Order Number DS21221
ISBN 0-86651-729-4

7 8 9 10 11 12-DR-04 03 02 01 00 99

DALE SEYMOUR PUBLICATIONS
P.O. BOX 10888
PALO ALTO, CA 94303

This book is printed on recycled paper.

Contents

Introduction

Problem Play is a collection of forty problems designed to develop childrens' problem-solving skills. They require children to think both logically and creatively; they reward systematic thought, a willingness to be wrong, and an eye for pattern. Some of the problems can be solved only through careful deliberation. Others have solutions that will pop out to children in a sudden burst of insight. All will increase a child's appreciation for and understanding of mathematical ways of thinking.

About the book

Each problem appears on a separate reproducible student page. The students will cut some of these pages; others they will use to record their answers. On the back of each student page is a discussion of the problem for the teacher. The directions to children for each problem are to be read aloud to the class. Lists of materials, prerequisite language and concepts, suggestions for getting started on the solution, the answer, and notes on the problem, including interesting features and the mathematical underpinnings of the problem, are also provided for the teacher. Each discussion concludes with a section on suggestions for follow-up activities to extend the problem into more difficult challenges.

Using the problems

The problems are arranged so that the easiest ones tend to be grouped toward the beginning, and the harder, more time-consuming problems appear toward the end. More important than a problem's level of difficulty, however, is how it can be integrated into a curriculum. Many of the problems fit a theme, such as castles, pizza, Valentine's Day, or insects, and can be integrated easily into the rest of the children's studies.

Though an excellent source of enrichment activities for strong students, the book is equally useful for less able children. The first grader who adds slowly and laboriously on his fingers may turn out to have a deeper insight into geometry than anyone else in the class. The second grader who hates the rote work of addition facts may be energized when she discovers that these problems make her use her creativity, as well as her memory. The persistence and understanding of some of the quieter students in solving these problems is impressive. Children who do not usually stand out in math often get a chance to shine in this kind of work.

While these problems work well as individual assignments, with each child working on the problem alone, this is by no means the only way to use this book with a primary grade class. Having children work in pairs can help alleviate frustration and increase insight; cooperative work allows children to bounce ideas off of each other and together arrive at a solution. Most of the problems can also be used as an exercise with the whole class, using manipulatives and large diagrams on a chalkboard or the floor.

Focus on problem-solving strategies

The problems in this book are intended to help you concentrate on the development of childrens' problem-solving skills, so the emphasis is always on solution strategies rather than on computational practice.

Difficult problems will require different strategies; often a problem can be solved in more than one way. Some of the strategies that students may find helpful are

Look for the pattern
Guess and test
Use logical reasoning
Draw a picture

Make an organized list
Make a table or a diagram
Use objects as models or act out the problem
Work backwards
Solve a simpler problem of the same sort

Suggestions for teaching problem solving

Problem solving should be a part of every student's daily work in math. Try to allow from ten to fifteen minutes every day for discussion and work on the problems. Few if any of the problems in this book are simple enough to be completed in a single ten-minute session, but that is as it should be. Such a schedule gives students time to think about the problem a bit, then leave it alone for a while and come back later with fresh ideas.

Here are some essential strategies to use in teaching problem solving.

Be actively involved with every problem. Before assigning a problem, solve it on your own. Make sure that you understand the directions thoroughly. What pitfalls will your students be likely to have? What background information should you go over first? Will it be helpful to take a small group aside to work on the problem together? In the follow-up discussion, by all means tell children about your own adventures in working through the problems—especially if it took you a while and you went down several blind alleys at first.

Define the problem. Carefully discuss the intent of each new problem when you introduce it. After you read the directions to the children, invite questions. Be sure to thoroughly discuss the necessary language and concepts listed on the teacher page. For students to succeed, it is essential that they understand what a problem is asking.

Answer questions with questions. As children work, they will no doubt have questions.

Whenever possible, answer their questions with questions of your own, or direct them to classmates. Ask, "Why do you think a 3 should go there?" or "What other ways are there to make a triangle?"

Allow students to devise their own plans. Different approaches to a problem are always possible. Let children come up with their own solving strategies. Follow-up discussions, group searches for patterns, and a class rehash of different solving methods are all tremendously valuable. Often children are astonished to find that classmates "did it differently."

Help students articulate general principles. Encourage children to generalize from their own work and the patterns that they see. For example, "You have to make the bottom corner green or you can't ever solve the problem." "There's always a diagonal line somewhere!"

Take time. It is also important to give children plenty of time to work a problem through. Putting a problem aside for a day may provide the spark needed to find a solution. Moreover, many of the problems ask for minimum or maximum answers. This takes more thought than finding one correct solution. Quick solvers can be asked, "Find a way of using even less" or can be questioned, "How do you know there could not be any more?" Math is more open-ended than children usually realize; there is rarely only one right way to solve a problem, and often several equally valid answers. This feature helps children develop a tolerance for ambiguity, which is tremendously important as they move through the grades.

Solving a problem may not always be fun; sometimes it is hard work. But the pleasure in reaching a successful solution generally makes the effort worthwhile. Problem solving can be a rich and satisfying facet of mathematics. Let your students discover its rewards.

Home, Sweet Home

1

Directions to Children
Four animals are trying to find their way home. Draw lines connecting each animal with its proper home. The lines may not touch or cross another animal's home. In particular, no line may go under the fishbowl. All lines must stay inside the house outline, except for the bird, which flies down the chimney.

Materials
Pencils and the problem sheet, or blackboard and chalk, or string and a large area (see Notes).

Necessary Language and Concepts
Crossing, touching, around, under, inside, animal homes.

Getting Started
- Resolve the major difficulty created by the fish. A line directly from the fish to the fishbowl cuts off the spider and the dog from their homes. A solution necessarily involves somebody detouring to accommodate everybody.
- See that one path necessarily affects the placement of another path.

Answer
The problem has two basic solutions, the difference being whether the dog's path goes to the right or the left of the spider web.

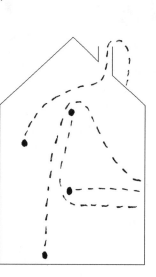

Notes
- This problem is well suited to solving as a group; for one thing, group work prevents the multiple erasures that scratch holes through paper. An approximate outline can be chalked onto the floor or taped onto the rug. Children can then represent the animals and the homes. Pieces of yarn may be laid on the floor to make the paths. The idea of cooperation can be strengthened, particularly if you start by asking the fish how to get home; that child most likely will take the shortest path. Should the fish have to go around just because somebody else cannot make it home?
- The problem has no numbers to confuse mathophobes.

Going Beyond
- Switch the positions of the dogbed and the spider web, or the fishbowl and the bird cage. Is the problem still possible?
- Give children an outline of the house. Have them draw in their own animals and place their homes anywhere in the outline. They then can solve the problem themselves or exchange with a classmate to solve.

Buzzing Away

3

Directions to Children

The hexagonal grid represents a beehive. One bee can live in each hexagon. A family of bees is to move in. Unfortunately, the bees do not like each other very much, so no two can live in adjacent spots. How many bees altogether can fit into this hive?

Materials

Counters or construction paper circles as wide as the small hexagons; the problem sheet; crayons or markers for coloring in the final product.

Necessary Language and Concepts

Next to; apart.

Getting Started

- Have patience. Plunking down chips at random will rarely give children the maximum answer. Children who do well at this problem take their time and shift chips around to try to open new places for other bees.
- Recognize that not all spaces are created equal. In particular, the very top and bottom hexagons are valuable because placing a bee in one of them eliminates only one adjacent space from consideration. Other squares toward the top, however, are undesirable because they border on six different spaces. A maximum solution to the problem makes heavy use of hexagons that do not border many others.

Answer

Several of these can be moved to produce slightly different maximum results.

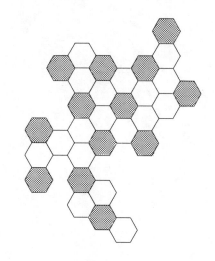

Notes

- Minimum or maximum problems like this can be either frustrating or liberating to children, because there is no obvious moment when the problem has suddenly been solved. Extremely frustrated children may be told the maximum answer (13) and can be challenged to find a way of arranging that many, but for most children the task of finding an appropriate stopping point is an appropriate additional challenge.

Going Beyond

- If you were allowed to add one new hexagon anywhere, where would you put it? Can you get to 15 bees by adding just one new hexagon?
- If the bees were really unfriendly, they would arrange themselves so that nobody new could get in. How few bees can you put into the spaces so that there is no room for anybody else without somebody moving?

Pizza for Lunch

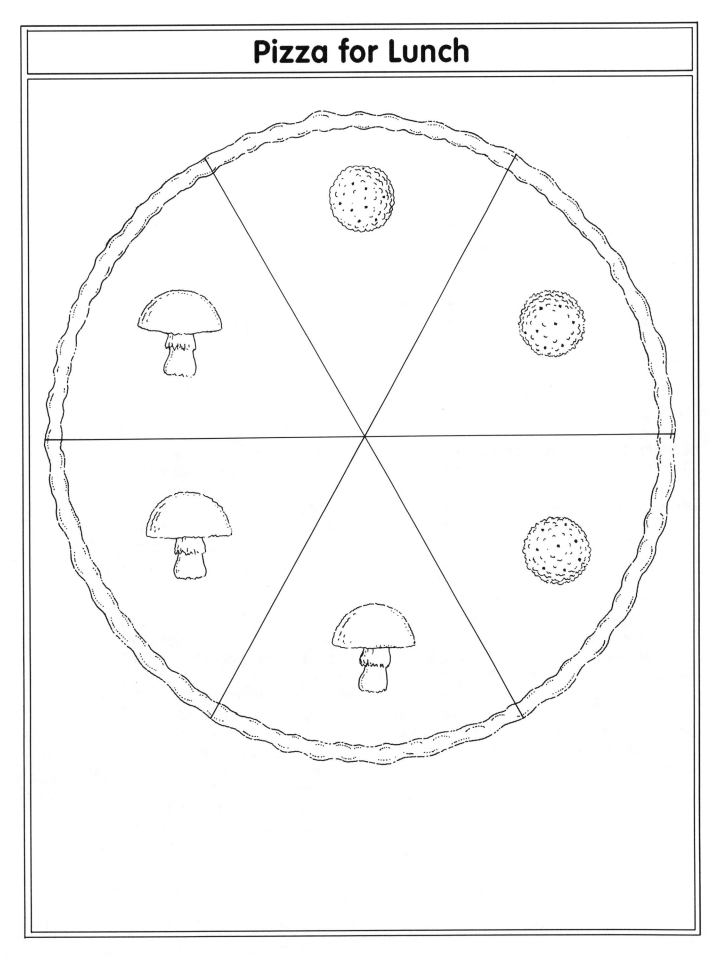

Directions to Children

This is a 6-slice pizza. Cut out the pieces. Place them so that one side of the pizza has three sausage slices, and the other side has three mushroom slices. By making exactly two switches, rearrange the pieces so that the slices alternate sausage-mushroom-sausage-mushroom all around the pizza. To make one switch, pick up any two slices and switch their positions. Remember to make exactly two switches, no more and no less.

Materials

The problem sheet; checkers or chips of contrasting colors to represent the pizza slices can be used.

Necessary Language and Concepts

Alternating; switching; no more, no less.

Getting Started

- Stop and think. The problem with making switches at random is that children are limited to a specific number of moves. After choosing a first move, it is essential for solvers to look for a switch that will solve the problem right away; some children forget.
- Avoid preconceptions. Some children see a one-move answer right away—switching the middle sausage for the middle mushroom. That answer does not follow the rules, though. Children who find that switch need to be able to try something else or to see how it can be combined with another move to solve the problem.

Answer

There are many possible answers. Trade 1 and 2, 4 and 5 or Trade 6 and 3, 2 and 4.

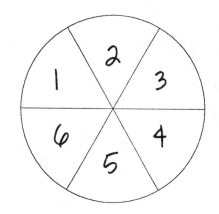

Notes

- No matter what the first switch is, the problem can be solved on the second move. No rule says that two mushroom slices cannot be exchanged for each other or that one slice cannot be switched twice. The purpose of the two-switch rule is to direct children away from the most obvious solution and to lead them toward other, less obvious possibilities.

Going Beyond

- Draw a five-piece pizza—two sausage, three mushroom. Try the problem again. How many moves does it take this time? Why is it impossible?
- Try it with an eight-piece pizza. Can it be done in two moves now?
- A similar problem can be done with a certain number of cups in a row, some right side up, some upside down. Two at a time may be turned over. The object is to get them all upright at the end of a turn. Children can explore the question. Under what circumstances is this possible? The key to this problem is whether the number of cups upside down at the start is even or odd.

Be My Valentine

Directions to Children

Cut out the circle and the square. Put them together to form a heart. Either or both of the shapes may be cut, but you are limited to no more than four cuts altogether.

Materials

Scissors, tape, and the problem sheet.

Necessary Language and Concepts

"Fitting together" is just as in a jigsaw problem: no overlap and no wide spaces between pieces.

Getting Started

- Think about differences between curves and straight lines.
- Recognize that the heart is exactly as large as the combined area of the square and circle.
- Be willing to play with the shapes and not to give up easily.

Answer

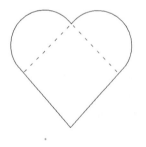

Notes

- The heart is not *mathematically correct,* because of the straight lines on the side. Kindergartners and first graders can solve the problem rather easily by using the drawing of the heart. Above first grade, the problem becomes almost trivial; children should be given just the circle and the square and should be challenged to transform the two into one heart-shaped figure. If children have trouble because they expect a heart to have no straight lines, it may be helpful to draw on the chalkboard an oversized version of the one from the problem sheet.
- The "four cuts" restriction is necessary because of the children who will chop up the shapes into 24 pieces and tape them randomly within the heart figure.

Going Beyond

- What other shapes can be formed under the rules?
- Do sizes matter? Try the problem with an enlarged circle.
- Is it easier to work the problem forward—according to the rules—or backward—cutting the heart and fitting together the pieces to form a square and a circle? (Interested children might like to take the problem home and compare results.)

Geometry, Mental flexibility

Up, Down, and Across

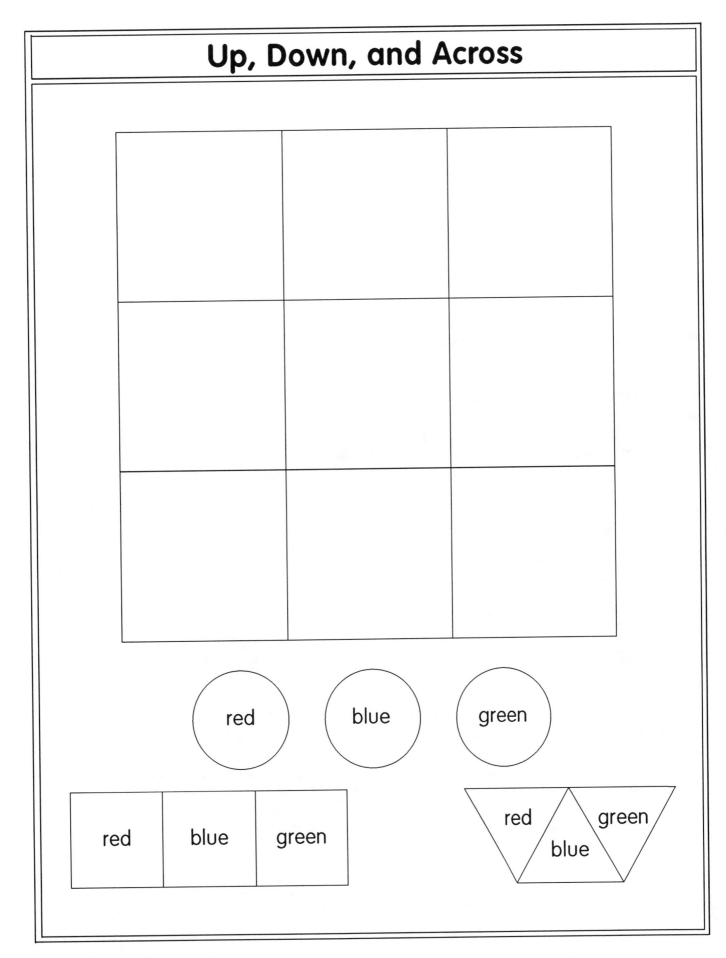

Directions to Children

Color the shapes at the bottom of the page, and cut them out. Place the shapes in the diagram, one to a square. No row may have the same shape or color twice; putting a green circle in the upper left corner, for instance, means that no more greens or circles are allowed in the top row. The same is true for the columns. How can all 9 pieces be placed?

Materials

The problem sheet, scissors, markers or crayons, tape or glue.

Necessary Language and Concepts

Same and different; rows and columns. It is helpful to run through a few group activities before introducing the problem itself: "Which boxes are in the first row?" "Find a column." "What pieces have something (color or shape) in common with the blue square?" "What pieces are not like the blue square in any way?"

Getting Started

- Keep two attributes in mind at once. After a few pieces have been placed, things get complicated. Many children forget either shape or color as they work.
- Check your work. It is easy to make mistakes, but they are easy to catch if children go through their finished work step by step, checking every row and then every column, to make sure that every shape and color is there.
- Use a method. This problem has an interesting feature. If you start in the upper left corner and work through the problem row by row, you will get a complete solution, guaranteed, as long as you follow the rules at every step. The same is true if you work shape by shape, column by column, or color by color. Children who start by putting down

three or four random pieces on scattered parts of the grid almost always run into a contradiction.

Answer

Other solutions can be obtained by trading; trade all blues for the same shape greens; trade all circles for squares of the same color.

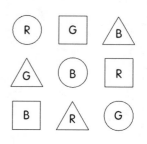

Notes

- Any problem involving attributes sharpens childrens' flexibility of thought. A blue triangle has to be treated as a blue piece, but it is also a triangle. The ability to keep two attributes in mind at once is important in many math topics—place value, factors and multiples, and area and perimeter are just a few.
- Every move made affects the placement of the next piece. This problem is a good example of the interconnections in mathematics.

Going Beyond

- Explore the diagonals. (In every solution, one diagonal is all one color and the other is all one shape.) Can you find a pattern?
- Try four shapes and four colors on a 4 x 4 grid, following the same rules. It is more complicated, but the patterns are wonderful.

Tree Triangles

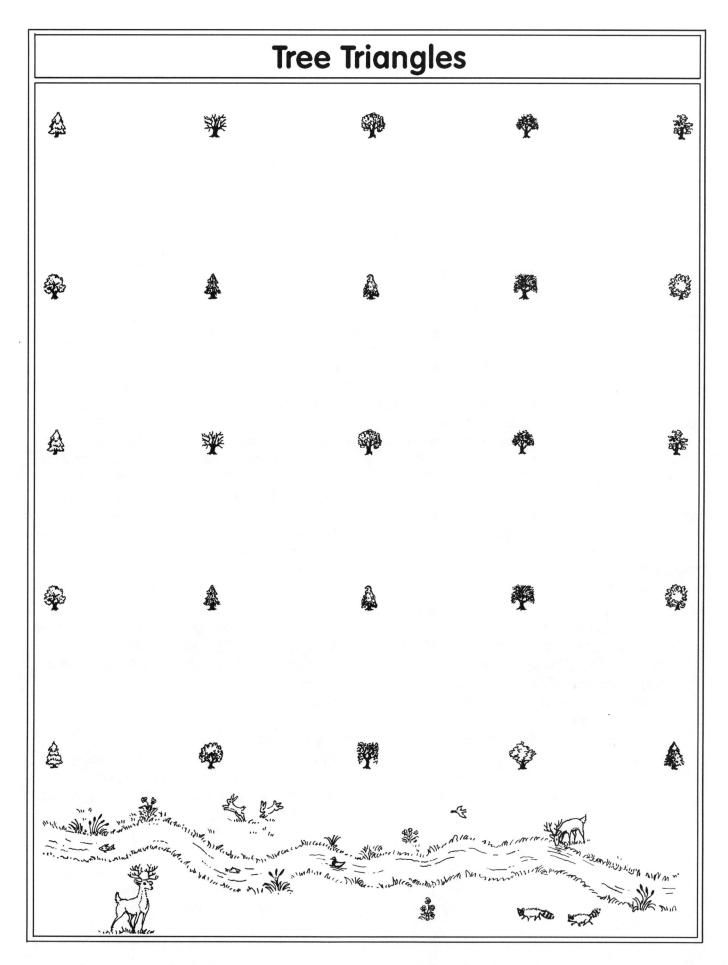

Directions to Children

The 25 trees are neatly planted in rows. We are going to loop string around these trees and make as many triangles as we can. Inside each triangle, we will plant a different color of flower. The triangles may not touch or cross each other, and no tree may be used for more than one triangle. How many triangles are possible? Remember that there are many different shapes for triangles.

Materials

This problem works very well with rubber bands and a 5 x 5 geoboard. Otherwise use pencil, the problem sheet, and perhaps crayons or markers for coloring in the triangles to represent the color of the flowers that will be planted there.

Necessary Language and Concepts

"Triangle" as a shape with three lines and three angles, or turns; the many shapes and sizes of triangles; touching and crossing.

Getting Started

- Realize that, in general, large triangles mean fewer triangles. This is intuitive for a good many children but not for all.
- Be willing to experiment. Odds are good that a child's first solution will not be the best solution, because a few trees probably will be unused and scattered around the grid. How can the triangles be moved, if only slightly, to accommodate another one somewhere in the problem?

Answer

This is one of many answers.

Notes

- Many children will start drawing in triangles and get stuck after about five or six. Either the remaining trees are too far apart to connect, or the triangles are too big and go right past some trees that could be used for other triangles. Of the two, the first is by far the easier to fix. The best solution has eight triangles, with seven triangles containing exactly three dots. The eighth either includes four dots or three dots, and one dot is left over. On a board with *m* rows of *n* trees, the general formula for the maximum number of triangles is given by (*m* x *n*) divided by 3, with the remainder ignored. In specific cases, though, the configuration of the dots reduces the number of triangles. On a 3 x 3 geoboard, for instance, it should be possible to get in three triangles, but it is not.

Going Beyond

- Add one dot below the one on the lower left. Does this add to the number of triangles? Add another dot below that one. How about now? Try removing a dot, making 24. What other arrangements of 24 are possible? Do they all have the same maximum answer? How many triangles can you get if you leave the unused tree in the middle of a triangle, not simply along its edge?

Across the USA

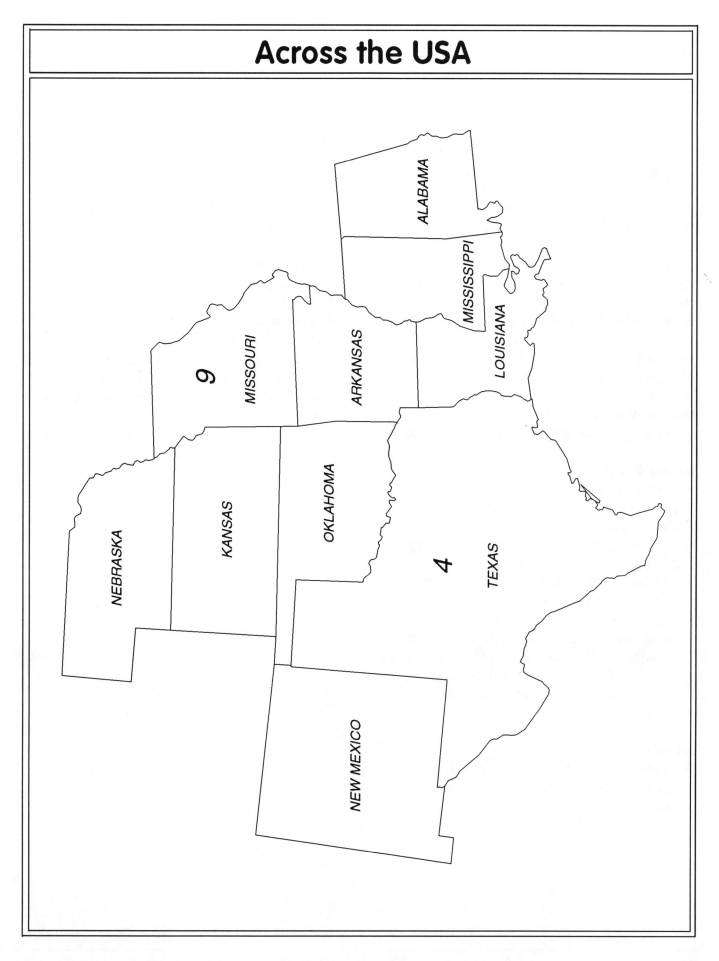

Directions to Children

A family went on a tour by car of ten states. They started in one state and went through the other nine one by one, never going back into a state they had already been in. Unfortunately, the trip was a long time ago, and the family cannot remember the order in which they went through the states. They did remember, though, that Texas was fourth and Missouri was ninth. Number the states from one to ten to show the order the family visited them.

Materials

Pencil and the problem sheet.

Necessary Language and Concepts

Never going back into a state already visited.

Getting Started

- Use the fact that Alabama connects to only one other state in the diagram. Because Mississippi cannot come both before and after Alabama, Alabama must either begin or end the tour. Because Missouri was next-to-last and does not border Alabama, Alabama must be first.
- Recognize that some possible orders will isolate some states. Going from Texas to Oklahoma, for instance, makes it impossible to get to New Mexico except by ending the journey there, as New Mexico does not border anything else.

Answer

Alabama, Mississippi, Louisiana, Texas, New Mexico, Oklahoma, Kansas, Nebraska, Missouri, Arkansas.

Notes

- This problem is related to the bridge problem on page 31. Each asks children to construct a path that makes it possible to get from one place to another. This one, however, has only one solution.

Going Beyond

- Suppose Arkansas were number 4 and Nebraska were 9. What route would work?
- Are there any states that cannot be on the end—neither first nor last?
- Using a big map of the United States, try planning a 48-state tour following the rules. Many ways are possible. Where do all of them either begin or end?

Ants, Ants, Ants

Directions to Children

Six ants live in the six houses, one in each. They would love to visit each other, but first they have to build roads between the houses so that each ant has a road that goes directly to the house of each other ant. Although you will see all kinds of interesting paths that can be drawn between any two houses, you should draw in only one, the straightest possible. How many roads are needed to connect each pair of ants?

Materials

Pencil, the problem sheet, and a ruler. The problem is easy to represent on a geoboard or with people as the ants and string as the roads.

Necessary Language and Concepts

Connecting; straight; a road for each pair of ants.

Getting Started

- Find a system. It can be easy to lose track of what already has been done without drawing the roads in some kind of order. Using a system also can help children know when to quit—a sticking point in problems that ask for a minimum or maximum.
- Use the visual clues to help in finding patterns. The finished network of roads is not only symmetric but is familiar to children. This pattern begins to reveal itself early on, and it can really help alert children to where new lines ought to be. Good problem-solvers use all sorts of evidence in their work.

Answer

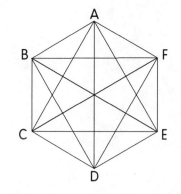

Notes

- This is a version of what mathematics calls the Handshake Problem. If each person in a room shakes hands with everybody else, how many handshakes have there been altogether? (It can be fun to try this out on a rainy day.) In the ant-and-house problem, ant A needs five roads, one to each of the other boxes. Ant B needs only four more roads, because a road already links B with A. Ant C needs three, and so on. The total is given by 5 + 4 + 3 + 2 + 1. In general, with n ants, the formula is $(n - 1) + (n - 2) + . . . + 1$. Another way to express this would be half of $[n \times (n - 1)]$.

Going Beyond

- This problem leads to many *creative math* projects. Are more roads connecting with A or with E?
- How about recasting the problem with 4, 5, or 7 ants?
- Make a table showing the number of roads for each given number of ants. What patterns are evident in the numbers in the table? What happens to the visual pattern of roads on the paper?

Tic-Tac-Toe, Two Turns to Go

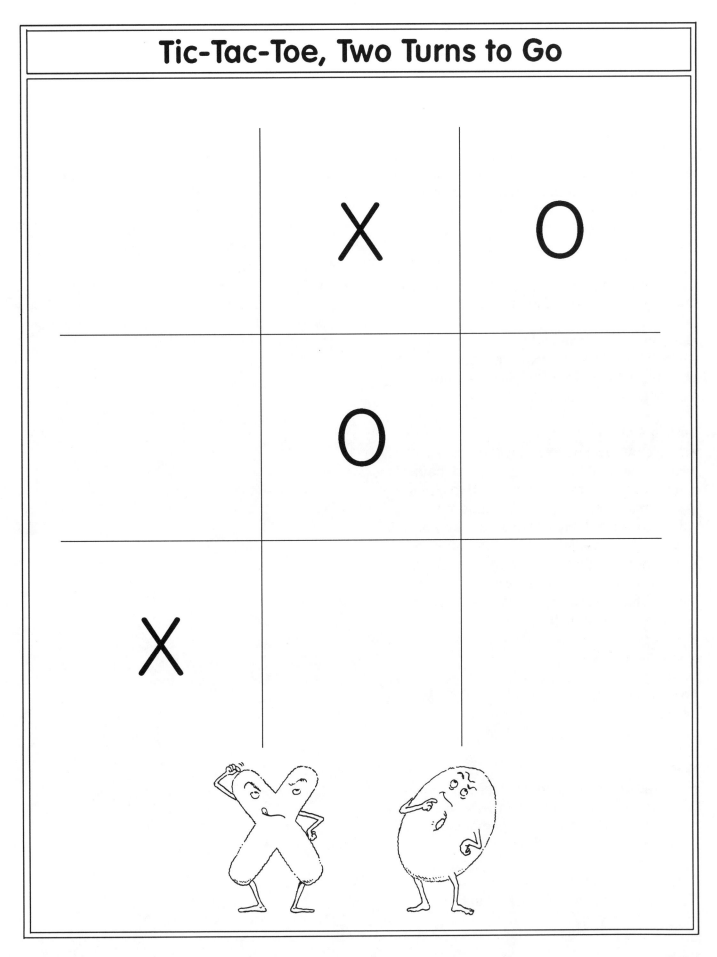

Directions to Children
This is a Tic-Tac-Toe game in progress. It is O's turn to play. O cannot win on its next turn, but it wants to put itself into position to win on the turn after that. Where should O play to be sure of winning the game?

Materials
Pencil and the problem sheet; a set of cutout O's and X's are a good idea.

Necessary Language and Concepts
Children should be familiar with the rules and object of Tic-Tac-Toe. They also need to have the concept of diagonals.

Getting Started
- Use strategy. In a two-player game, strategy essentially means thinking beyond the next turn. O has four moves that lead to a possible win on the next turn. The catch is to identify the moves that allow O to win in two possible ways, making it impossible for X to block.
- Put yourself into the other player's shoes. What will X's next move be? Children may forget that X also is playing to win; it is helpful to remind them as they work.
- Recognize that three in a row also applies to the diagonals.

Answer
Either the space adjacent to the two circles, or the space directly below that one.

Notes
- Tic-Tac-Toe is a game much analyzed by mathematicians. If each player uses the best strategy at the start of the game, the game will end in a draw. In the example here, X obviously has made some mistake. More complicated games, like chess, are still awaiting complete analysis of this kind.

Going Beyond
- Have a Tic-Tac-Toe tournament. Can any player figure out a strategy to guarantee winning or drawing every game?
- What if it were X's turn to play right now instead of O's? What is X's best move? What chance of winning does X have if O does not make a mistake?
- Try Tic-Tac-Toe on a 4 x 4 geoboard. Does it make any difference who goes first? Try a few games, and keep track of whether the first or second player wins more often.

Malicious Fish

19

Directions to Children

Malicious Fish—a rare species—is swimming in its tank. As the name implies, it is not a good idea to put more than one in the same tank. Just for fun, though, suppose that the tank were filled with Malicious Fish. How many fish can fit in the tank without any of the fish overlapping? The only tool you may use is the cut out tank from the problem sheet itself.

Materials

Scissors to cut out the tank, the problem sheet, and nothing else.

Necessary Language and Concepts

Touching; the cut out tank can be a tool.

Getting Started

- Use visual clues to estimate. Most children will measure by eye and decide that one fish can fit under the present one and another can fit directly to the left of it. As they get farther from the fish, children can lose track of how big the fish actually is. More successful solvers rely on their visual sense and refer to the drawing often.
- Find a way of measuring without any outside tools. Even if children make use of their fingers or spots on the desk, they still must measure accurately—not the easiest of jobs.

Answer

Eight

Notes

- The trick to solving this problem makes it unnecessary to estimate or to find a more or less accurate measuring device; it involves the paper itself and is the reason why the directions should stress that the sheet is a tool. Once the students have cut out the tank, they can fold it in half lengthwise. It will be clear that as many fish will be on the right side as on the left. From there it is an easy step to fold the paper twice more horizontally. Unfolding the paper reveals eight boxes, each exactly the size of the Malicious Fish.

Going Beyond

- Estimate all sorts of things: how many blocks it would take to stretch from one end of the room to the other, how many sheets of paper will cover a table, how long a piece of string must be to encircle a group of children sitting on the floor.
- Measure all sorts of things: the width of the classroom, the heights of the students, the length of everybodys' hair.

Money in the Bank

Discussion for **Money in the Bank**

Directions to Children

This figure looks like a pie with a large slice cut out, but it is actually a bank. The bank is to be filled with pennies, nickels, dimes, and quarters. Coins may touch the outlines of the bank, but no part of a coin may cross the line or overlap another coin. Your job is not to fill the bank with the most coins but rather to fill the bank with coins that will equal the greatest possible amount of money.

Materials

Coins (fake coins are fine as long as they are the right sizes), the problem sheet, and a sharp pencil to draw in the outlines of the money.

Necessary Language and Concepts

Outline, overlapping. Children must be able to identify the coins, know their values, and sum the total.

Getting Started

- Mentally weigh the value of the coins against the size. On the one hand, it is possible to fit more pennies into the bank than nickels, but on the other hand, one nickel is worth five pennies. Are you better off with bigger, more valuable coins, or with smaller but less valuable ones?

- In particular, realize the importance of dimes. A dime is more valuable than a penny or a nickel; it is also smaller. Any solution containing pennies or nickels can immediately be made more valuable by changing those coins for dimes.

- Start with an area of the bank restricted by the outline and work in. Starting at the middle may be very successful but also may result in lots of empty space when children finally reach the edge of the outline and find not even enough room for a dime.

Answer

The answer depends on dexterity and exact definition of where the lines begin and end. A reasonable answer is 21 quarters and 3 dimes, worth $5.55.

Notes

- Even with pennies and nickels eliminated from the bank (and not all children will do this by any means), the issue of dimes versus quarters remains thorny. A quarter is worth 250% of a dime but is less than 250% bigger; therefore, quarters are a wiser choice. This is by no means obvious, however, and may lead to some interesting discussions in the classroom.

Going Beyond

- The shape of the bank affects the answer. What if it were a complete circle or another shape entirely? What if it were irregular?

- Is it easier to do the problem with curved outlines or straight ones? Why?

- Some children may notice that a dime is thinner than a quarter. This makes the difference in volume much less than the difference in area. A barrel of dimes may actually be more valuable than a barrel of quarters.

Addition, Part/whole relationships

$$\cap\cap''''' = 25$$

$$\cap\cap\cap\cap\cap\cap\cap'' = 72$$

$$ee\cap''''''' = 218$$

$$e\cap\cap\cap\cap'''' = \underline{}$$

$$\underline{} = 62$$

Discussion for **Cleopatra's Arithmetic Book**

Directions to Children

The three examples show how the ancient Egyptians wrote the numbers 25, 72, and 218. What number does the next Egyptian symbol represent? How would the Egyptians have written the number 62?

Materials

The problem sheet and a pencil.

Necessary Language and Concepts

Recognition of our (Arabic) numerals through the 100s place.

Getting Started

- Recognize that the symbols used by the Egyptians were not purely random but actually stood for something.
- Realize that the Egyptian numbers are produced by adding the symbols together, unlike in our system, but that the Egyptian system is a decimal base, like ours.

Answer

ℯ∩∩∩∩'''' = 144 ∩∩∩∩∩∩'' = 62
(ℯ = 100, ∩=10, ' = 1)

Notes

- This actually is the system used by ancient Egyptians. The system can provide a nice transition into the study of place value; children can adjust easily to the symbols and accept that the inverted U stands for 10.
- Although the Egyptian system is in many ways more cumbersome than ours, it is easier in several respects. Subtraction, for instance, is simple cancellation, and regrouping is especially easy. For children who have difficulty with regrouping, it can be helpful to translate a problem into Egyptian notation, regroup, solve, and then write the Arabic notation for each step on the side.

Going Beyond

- Which is easier to work with, the Egyptian system or ours? Why?
- What do you think they did when they got up to 1,000?

Fish, Fresh Fish

__ + __ + __ + __ = 15

Directions to Children
You are going fishing. Catch exactly four fish that will weigh exactly 15 pounds in all. Each fish has its weight marked on its back, so you know right away whether to keep it or throw it back. What combination of four fish will reach exactly 15 pounds? Each fish, of course, can only be used once.

Materials
Paper and the problem sheet. Some children like to use Cuisenaire® rods of the lengths representing the fishes' weights.

Necessary Language and Concepts
Sums to ten; exactly four fish; once and only once.

Getting Started
- Use the three-pound fish. The problem may be solved in several ways, but all of them include the three-pounder. The "catch" is that all the other fish weigh an even number of pounds, and no matter how many times you add up even numbers, you will never get an odd number like 15; an odd number must be somewhere in the bunch.

Answer
Possible answers 8 + 3 + 2 + 2; 3 + 4 + 4 + 4; 6 + 4 + 2 + 3.

Notes
- That two even numbers always add up to another even number is a delightful quirk of number theory and an excellent tool to work on pattern recognition and generalization with children. Children can begin by checking simple even numbers and pooling their answers (which will always be even); they then can use calculators to check what happens if very large even numbers like 654, 908, 422 are added. Then, more or less convinced that there are no counterexamples, they can draw diagrams, match up blocks, or loop each other in pairs with string to heighten their understanding of why even numbers always add up to an even number, no matter what the numbers are.

Going Beyond
- What would happen if all the fish weighed odd amounts?
- Explore odd + odd, odd + even, odd + odd + odd, and so on.
- Make a list of other similar mathematical "rules" that always work. Some suggestions: any number plus zero; any number minus itself; the pattern in the ones digit when you count by fives; commutativity of addition.

Caterpillars' Evening Out

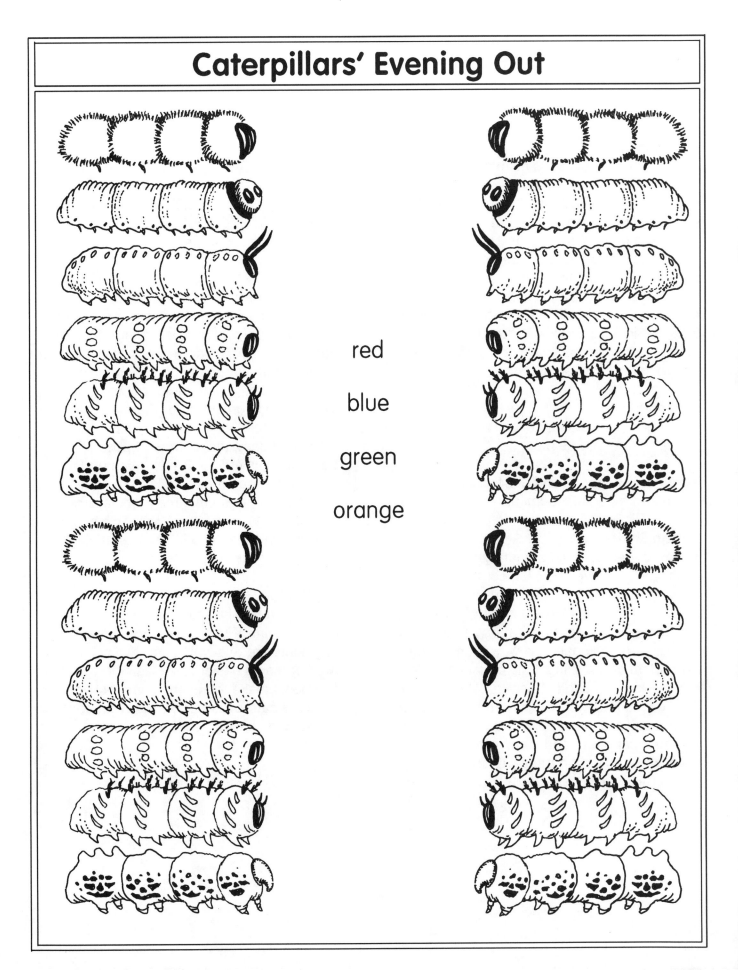

red

blue

green

orange

27

Directions to Children

A family of caterpillars is heading for a party. Each caterpillar must get dressed in four different colors—red, blue, green, orange. The colors may go in any order, but all four segments of a caterpillar must have different colors: for instance, red, blue, red, green is not allowed. Unfortunately, caterpillars are jealous of how they look. They refuse to appear in public looking exactly like another caterpillar. If they cannot find a new combination of clothing, they will just not go. How many of these 24 caterpillars will be able to go?

Materials

Crayons or markers in the four colors. Circles of colored paper are helpful.

Necessary Language and Concepts

Same and different; segments of a caterpillar.

Getting Started

- Find patterns. While a primary-grade child is unlikely to come up with a complete system for finding answers, children will do well if they can use any kind of a pattern at all. Finding all the possible caterpillars with blue heads, for instance, is a way of analyzing the problem and making it more manageable.

- Keep track of earlier answers. This is another way that finding a pattern can help. It is easy for a child to come up with six or seven random answers and then, forgetting the first answers, fill up the page with the same caterpillars all over again.

Answer

ROGB, ROBG, RBOG, RBGO, RGOB, RGRO, ORGB, ORBG, OBGR, OBRG, OGBR, OGRB, GBOR, GBRO, GORB, GOBR, GROB, GRBO, BGOR, BGRO, BROG, BRGO, BORG, BOGR. These can, of course, be listed in any order.

Notes

- This problem is an examination of permutations—the number of ways a given number of objects can be arranged. In this case, each caterpillar may choose any of four colors for its head, any of the three remaining for the next segment, either of two remaining for its third segment, and whatever is left over goes onto the tail.

- Mathematically, the number of possible caterpillars is $4 \times 3 \times 2 \times 1$, which equals 24; they all can go. In general, with n colors and n caterpillar segments, the formula is given by $n \times (n-1) \times (n-2) \ldots \times 1$. This number is called n factorial, and it is written $n!$ Children often get a kick out of that notation.

Going Beyond

- It can be fun to investigate other combinations. Three colors and three segments are relatively easy, two colors and two segments easier still. Five colors and five segments make things more interesting—120 possible caterpillars that way! What about six colors and six-segment caterpillars?

Don't Fence Me In

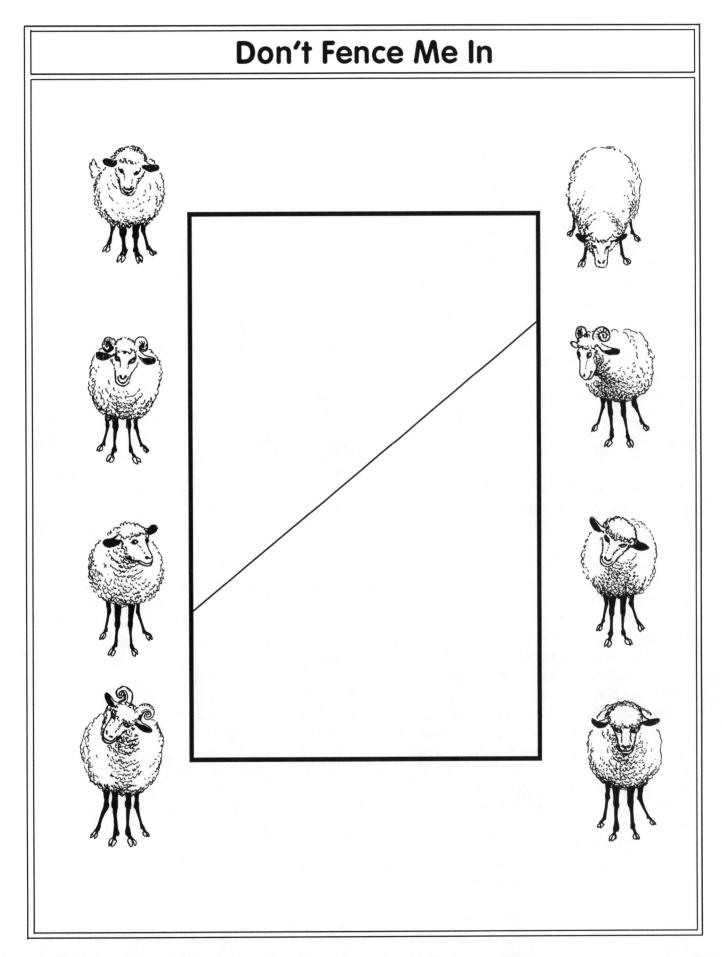

Directions to Children

The big rectangle is a sheep pen. I would like to keep lots of sheep in it, but I only have four fences, and each sheep needs a space of its own. I can stretch a fence from one edge of the pen to another but only in a straight line; the fences are allowed to cross. The first fence has been drawn in. When all the fences have been drawn, how many sheep can I fit? Their spaces do not have to be the same size.

Materials

Pencil, the problem sheet, and a straightedge. Small objects to represent sheep are nice but not necessary. The problem also lends itself to cooperative group work at a table with tape or string, especially for children who do not have good small muscle skills.

Necessary Language and Concepts

A sheep's *own space*, straight lines.

Getting Started

- Be willing to experiment. The second fence may be placed in an infinite number of ways. Is it better to place it near the edge of the pen or straight down the middle? Does it matter whether it crosses the first? Should the fences run parallel to one another? Children who examine each question in turn should come close to a maximum answer on this problem.
- Generalize from specific cases. A little thought demonstrates that the best placement for the second fence crosses the first fence. That produces space for four sheep rather than three. If crossing is a good move for the second fence, it may be a good strategy to use for the third fence as well.
- Remember that the spaces need not all be the same size. As with a few other problems in this book, it is important to stay focused on the rules.

Answer

One possible answer:

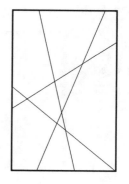

Notes

- The maximum answer, 11 sheep, is produced by crossing each fence through every previous fence. That adds as many new regions as there are lines. The fourth fence, for instance, cuts through four different spaces, adding four to the total. Beginning with one line, the sequence runs 2 regions, 4 regions, 7, 11. Adding a fifth line, assuming that you could draw it in accurately, would produce 16 spaces. The formula, with n fences, is $(1 + 2 + 3 + ... + n) + 1$. The final $+ 1$ seems strange, but remember that with no fences at all there is still room for one sheep.

Going Beyond

- Try it as a group with 1 fence, 2 fences, and so on, up to at least 4 or 5. Make a table that lists the number of fences and the number of sheep they would confine. Look for patterns. How far can you carry the table, even if you can no longer draw the figure? Any guesses what the figure would look like if you could draw 20 fences that each cross all the others?

Bridge Over the Water

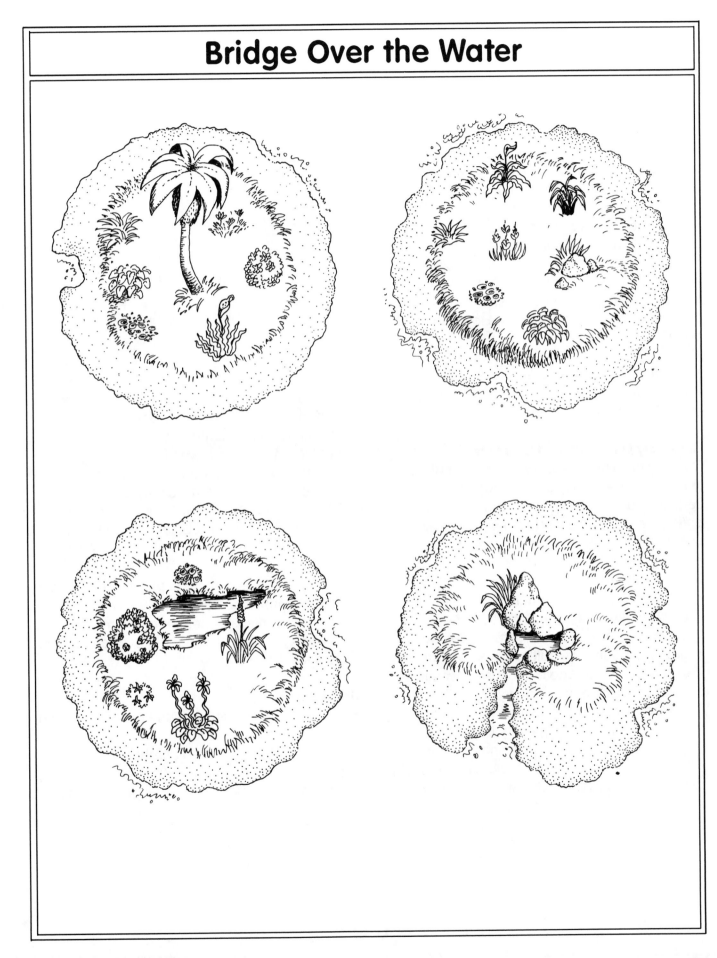

Directions to Children

Four small islands are in the middle of the Papyrus Sea. I am on the island with the palm tree. I would like to construct 7 bridges between the islands so that I can leave my island in the morning, cross each bridge exactly once, visit each of the other 3 islands, and return at the end of the day to my own home. It is okay to have 2 or more bridges going between the same 2 islands, or to have 2 islands that have no bridge linking them directly. How can this be done?

Materials

Pencil, the problem sheet, and 7 rods or craft sticks to represent bridges.

Necessary Language and Concepts

Connecting. The idea of *exactness* is critical to this problem—*exactly* seven bridges, visiting *each* island, crossing each bridge *once and only once.* It may be worth talking over this concept thoroughly before trying this problem.

Getting Started

- Be creative. Children often respond to this problem by thinking that it will be very easy, but some *obvious* solutions do not work.
- Understand the difficulties caused by having exactly seven bridges. Because seven is an odd number, many solutions that children try out first end up with the narrator crossing seven bridges, visiting every island, but winding up on a different island from the start. One bridge will need to be placed diagonally between two islands for the problem to work.
- Place the bridges in order, as though following a path, rather than placing the seven bridges and trying to find a way through them.

Answer

One possible answer:

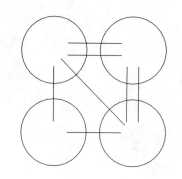

Notes

- This is similar to the famous Seven Bridges of Konigsberg problem, solved by the mathematician Leonhard Euler in the 18th century. Within the town of Konigsberg were seven bridges. The game in town was to devise a way to take a walk around the bridges, crossing each exactly once. No one was able to do it, and Euler proved it was impossible, given the configuration of the bridges.
- The key to this problem is placing the bridges so that each island has an even number of bridges. If this is done, the problem is always possible. If it is not done, the problem cannot be solved.

Going Beyond

- Draw circles and lines on the playground and walk across the bridges.
- Try the problem with a different number of bridges.
- Look at the Konigsberg problem (it can be found in many books on the history of math)—but do not try too long to solve it! You may like to figure out where an 8th bridge could go to make the problem solvable.

Reverse Word Search

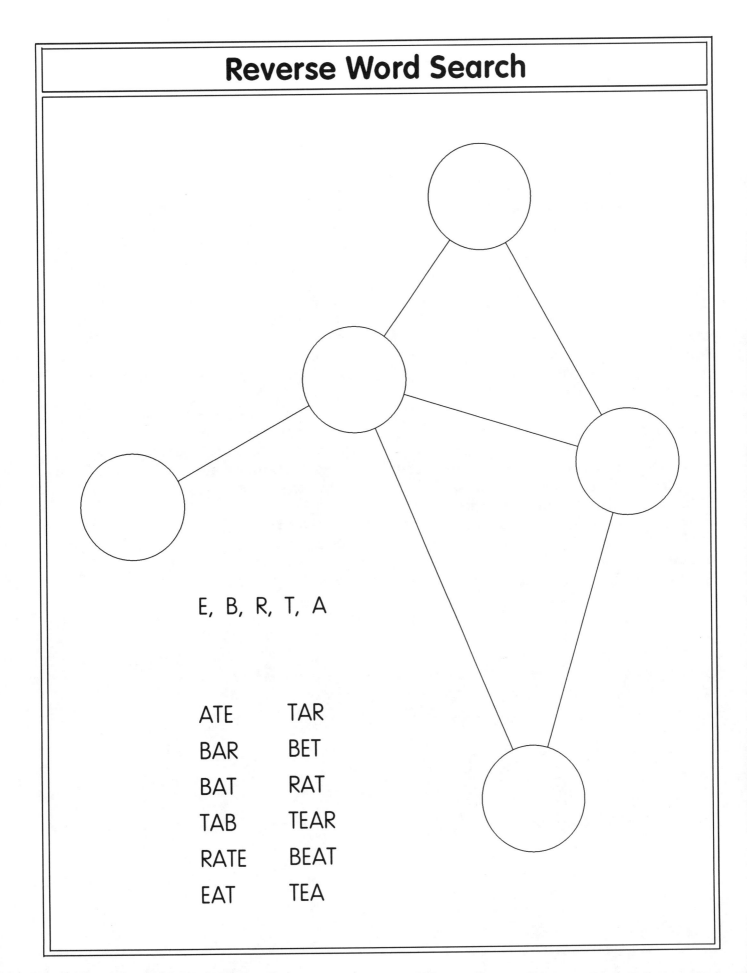

E, B, R, T, A

ATE   TAR
BAR   BET
BAT   RAT
TAB   TEAR
RATE   BEAT
EAT   TEA

Directions to Children

Put the five letters into the diagram, one in each circle, so that all of the listed words can be spelled out. Letters for each word must be connected in order by direct lines.

Materials

The problem sheet, a pencil, and small pieces of paper with the 5 letters written on them.

Necessary Language and Concepts

Next to, in order, connecting; spelling as a sequence of letters, although an ability to spell is actually not a prerequisite.

Getting Started

- Notice that some circles connect to more letters than others and that some letters need to connect to more letters than others.
- Check the word list carefully to make sure that all combinations are accounted for.

Answer

The problem has three solutions. The third solution is the second solution with T and B interchanged.

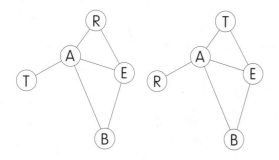

Notes

- Unfortunately, even on a first-grade level, some children hate numbers and anything having to do with them. This problem hides mathematical reasoning inside what looks like a perfectly ordinary word search. A child reluctant to try creative problems that involve numbers may be delighted to work on this one.
- It is possible to solve this problem by trial and error. In most cases, however, putting in letters at random will lead ultimately to a contradiction. Even trial-and-error solvers usually notice a pattern of some sort, such as the fact that the letter R needs to connect with only one other letter, and use it to find a complete solution.

Going Beyond

- Add an extra line on the grid. Does this add to the list of possible words?
- Try six letters and a six-circle diagram.

A Real Blockbuster

1   2   3   4   5   6   7   8   9   10

Discussion for **A Real Blockbuster**

Directions to Children
The tower is built from ten blocks. Number the blocks from one to ten, using the following rule: a block can rest only on a block with a lower number. For example, one cannot rest on two, but eight can rest on seven.

Materials
Pencil and the problem sheet. Cards with numbers on them or number tiles may be helpful.

Necessary Language and Concepts
On top of, under, resting on, more and less. It is a good idea to start with a quick project—on the board, using rods, or in the block area—that reviews the concept of *resting on*. For example, children might be asked to put together three rods so that the yellow and the red are both *resting on* the blue.

Getting Started
- Follow the rule. Forgetting it is the most common error in solving this problem. Remind children of the rule every so often as they work. This problem will not lead children to a contradiction if they break the rule, so it is also good to remind children that they ought to check their work as well.
- Recognize that the number of one block affects the placement of others. The problem is as delicate as the block tower; one misplaced number, and the whole thing comes crashing down.
- Start at the top or bottom and work in. The problem can be solved through trial and error by placing numbers like 5 and 6 in first, but the solution is far simpler to find for children who organize themselves and begin with high numbers at the top or low ones at the bottom.

Answer
This is one solution. All answers will have the 4, 9, and 10 in these positions.

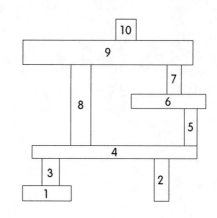

Notes
- The two long horizontal blocks are the keys to the problem and the main reason why only a few solutions are possible. They must contain the numbers 4 and 9. Group discussion of different answers should bring this to light.
- Have children count the blocks under the two long ones. What does this have to do with their numbers?

Going Beyond
- Design a different tower with 10 blocks. Give it to a friend to solve.
- Is a tower possible that has just one solution? How could you make a tower with the greatest number of solutions? What makes the two towers alike or different?

The Musical Snail

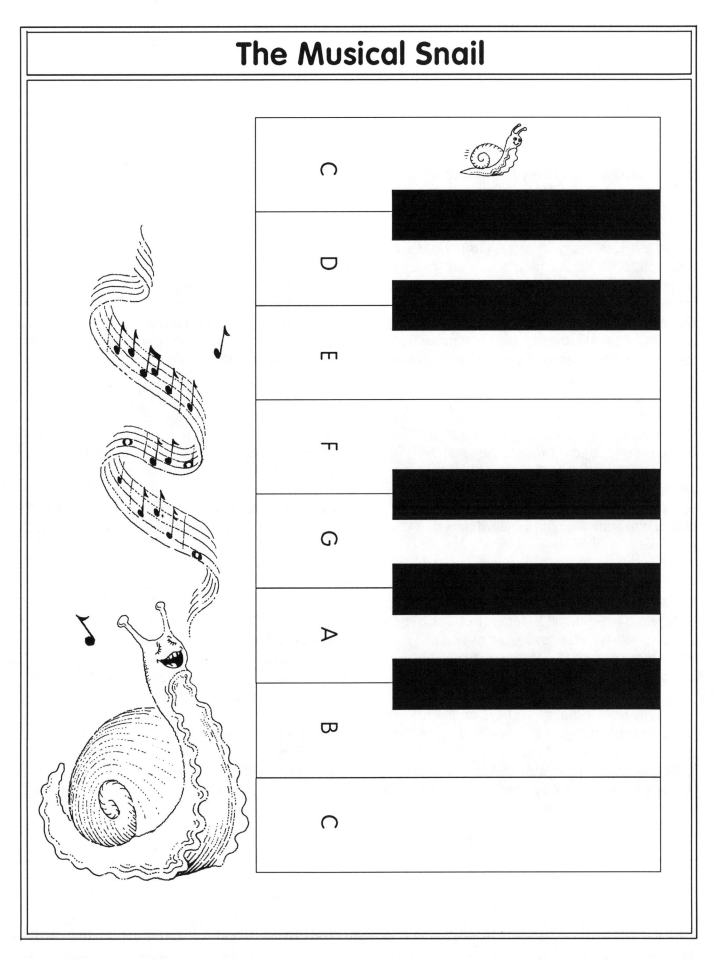

Directions to Children

The snail wants to go on vacation across the piano keyboard. Currently it is on middle C; it wants to get to high C. Snails move rather slowly, so the snail has planned to take four days to make the trip. Each day, however, it would like to move a different number of keys. If it moves four keys on the first day, for instance, it may never again move exactly four keys. The snail has only one problem—fear of high places. It refuses to end a day on one of the high black keys! How can the snail make it all the way to high C across the eleven intervening keys?

Materials

Pencil and the problem sheet; a bean or Cuisenaire® rod to represent the snail

Necessary Language and Concepts

Across; black and white keys (black keys are higher); exactly four days; four different numbers.

Getting Started

- Remember all the restrictions! Individually, they are not difficult to recall, but along the way children often lose sight of one or another of them.
- Use the restrictions to your advantage. Knowing that you cannot move the snail exactly one, three, or six keys on the first day eliminates many possibilities and simplifies the problem considerably.
- Recognize that the snail cannot cross too many keys in one day; there aren't enough keys for it to move all the way to the A the first time out!

Answer

Some possible answers:

Number of keys snail can go	(Notes)			
2 – 5 – 4 – 1	D	G	B	C
5 – 2 – 4 – 1	F	G	B	C
2 – 3 – 6 – 1	D	F	B	C

Notes

- This problem, like many problems in this book, has little overtly mathematical about it. It is designed to appeal particularly to students who like music, perhaps to the exclusion of math, though a child who has never seen a piano can solve this problem successfully too.
- Twelve moves are to be made altogether. On one level, the problem is simply finding four different numbers that add to 12 and then putting the numbers in order, in light of the restrictions on the black keys. Only two combinations are possible: 1, 2, 3, 6 and 1, 2, 4, 5. Each will work in the problem.

Going Beyond

- It can be fun to take all the possible solutions, find a piano, and play the four-note chord made up of the four keys on which the snail ends each of its days. Do any of the chords sound at all "musical"?
- Find four different numbers that add to make 12. Do you see the connection with this problem?
- What if the snail wanted to take just three days? How about five? (Five will not work. Can the children see why not?)

Points of the Star

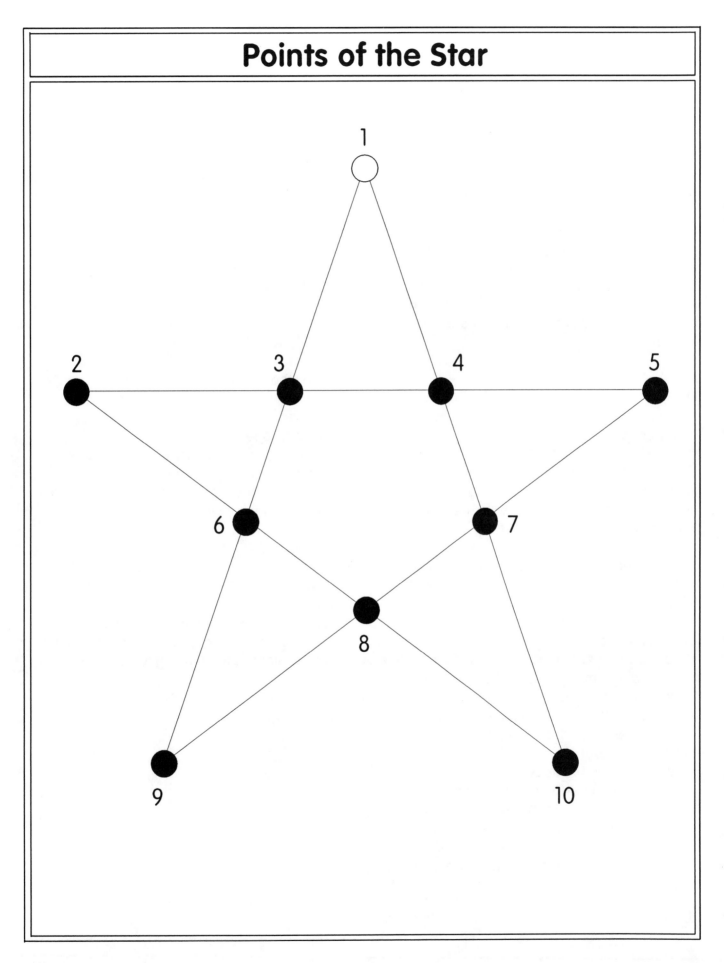

Directions to Children
The star has ten points where two lines intersect. Place counters on each of those points but the one marked "1." The object of the problem is to remove as many counters as possible. Counters are removed by being jumped. A piece may jump another if (a) the two pieces are adjoining and (b) an empty space is on the other side of the jumped piece. No piece may jump around a corner or over two pieces at once. In what order should the pieces be jumped?

Materials
Counters, the problem sheet, an extra sheet of paper to write down the sequence of moves, and a pencil.

Necessary Language and Concepts
Jumping, across, the same line, spaces that are next to one another. A good warm-up would involve locating numbers that are next to each other and along the same line without bending. This problem lends itself well to group solving with the diagram enlarged and placed on the floor.

Getting Started
- Recognize that the more pieces in the middle of the diagram, the better. Children often are inclined to try to get all their pieces to the points of the star. Unfortunately, pieces there cannot be jumped at all, while pieces in the middle can be.
- Take notes on the sequence of moves. Writing down the number of the piece moved is all that is really needed, but some system of record keeping is necessary so that work can be checked. Otherwise, children claim to have reduced the whole thing to no counters at all!

Answer
One way to end with just one counter is to move 6 to 1 (jumping over 3), move 10 to 6, move 9 to 3, move 4 to 10, move 2 to 4, move 1 to 7, move 10 to 4, move 5 to 3.

Notes
- Record keeping is an important part of mathematics, as indeed of most other subjects. Keeping even wrong or incomplete answers has value; this is one reason why writing teachers often ask students to hand in rough drafts, as well as finished products. A child who misses 6 addition problems out of 10 on a worksheet may be disappointed or embarrassed but can use those wrong answers to learn and to improve performance. The same is true with this problem; children can look back at an unsuccessful series of moves and figure out where they went wrong.

Going Beyond
- Does it matter where the empty space is to start? Leave number 8 blank, and try it that way.
- What is the largest number of pieces that can be left on the board so that no further jumps are possible? Can this position be reached?

The Square Table

Directions to Children

The four triangles are pieces of the top of a table shipped unassembled from the factory. The directions for assembly were not included with the package, but the table is supposed to be square. How can this be done? Cut out the triangles and put them together to form a square. Overlaps and spaces are not allowed.

Materials

The problem sheet, scissors, and tape.

Necessary Language and Concepts

Triangles; squares as figures with four equal sides and L-shaped corners; overlapping and spaces. It can be helpful to draw a few squares and non-squares on the board for children to categorize, including one or two squares whose sides are not parallel to the edges of the board.

Getting Started

* Be willing to try different ideas. Most children immediately see that two triangles make a square if the long ends are together. Unfortunately, the problem requires all four pieces, and there is no way to add the two remaining triangles so that the problem will work. The triangles may be connected in other ways, though, and a thorough solver will try one of these before long.
* Be flexible with the idea of a square. Depending on how the first triangle is oriented, children may put together a diamond and keep looking, thinking that a diamond is not a square. As long as the corners have the appropriate angle measurement, a diamond is a square. If children are still confused, have them rotate their diamonds (or themselves) or repeat the definition of a square, checking their figures as they go.

Answer

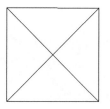

Notes

* Children often set up more rules in a problem than are actually there. In this case, there is no rule against having a tilted square, but many children will proceed as though that is forbidden. Several of these problems are designed so that a successful solver needs to question those assumptions and to discover what the problem really asks. Good mathematicians think creatively, and children cannot always do that when they are afraid of breaking the rules.
* The four triangles are isosceles—they have two equal sides and two equal angles. They are also right triangles—with an angle of 90 degrees. The problem is impossible with any other kind of triangle.

Going Beyond

* What other shapes can be made from these 4 triangles?
* Is it possible to make a square from 8 of the triangles? (Children can work together to investigate this one, pooling their problem sheets.)

Stop, Snakes!

Directions to Children

Four snakes have hidden behind the stop sign. Their heads and tails are colorless, but one has a red body and the other three are green. Although the green snakes do not touch or cross each other, the red snake crosses all three green ones. The snakes are pulled reasonably tightly; that is, they do not loop all over the place behind the sign but go more or less straight from head to tail. Which head goes with which tail, and what colors are the four snakes?

Materials

Pencil, crayons or markers, the problem sheet.

Necessary Language and Concepts

Crossing; straight; the idea that heads and tails must go together.

Getting Started

• Recognize that it is impossible for all four snakes to go across the center of the stop sign, so another solution must be found.

• Look for the possible snakes that do extend across the sign. In this diagram are two diagonals, and one of these must be the red snake. Any shorter snake could not cross all three of the others.

• Use symmetry. Although the symmetry in the problem may not be obvious, an accurate solution must include two short green snakes flanking a long green snake, all cut at right angles by the red snake.

Answer

The red snake may cross either diagonal.

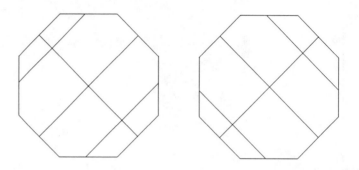

Notes

• The biggest sticking point in this problem is that the snakes can *go around the corner*—that is, the head on the extreme right can connect with the tail at the bottom of the diagram. Once it is drawn in, children usually can see that it will work, but until they see it, children are often loath to try any solution involving a head and tail that close together.

Going Beyond

• Play around with different arrangements of heads and tails. Some will work; some will not. (You might even try giving children one with five heads and three tails, just to see if anyone notices.)

• There are two blue snakes and two orange snakes. Each blue snake touches one of the orange snakes, but not both. How can this variation be solved?

Pick a Box, Any Box

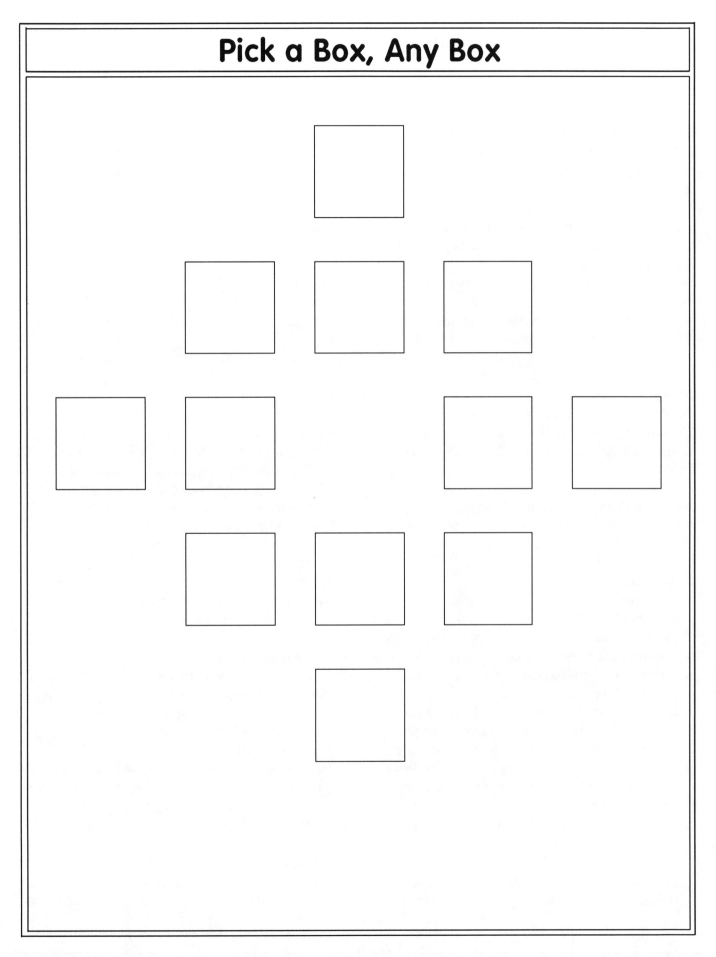

Directions to Children

Fill the 12 boxes with the numbers 2, 3, and 4. Four boxes will get a 2, four will get a 3, and four will get a 4. The numbers must be placed so that adjacent boxes contain consecutive numbers. A 2, for instance, can be placed next to a 3, but not next to a 4. Of course, a 2 cannot be placed next to another 2 either. In this problem, diagonal boxes are not considered adjacent to each other, and two boxes are not adjacent if their only connection is across the center space. How can the numbers be arranged according to the rules?

Materials

Pencil and the problem sheet. Dice, Cuisenaire® rods, number tiles, or scraps of paper with the numbers written on them are helpful.

Necessary Language and Concepts

Next to, adjacent; numbers being the same and different; consecutive numbers.

Getting started

- Be willing to question assumptions. The problem has multiple solutions, but all require the same placement of the threes. No matter how brilliant or hardworking a child may be, the problem is unsolvable with a three in the topmost box.
- Recognize that the three occupies a special role. Threes can be placed next to either of the other two numbers, while twos and fours can be placed only next to threes. The threes therefore must go in the most central of the boxes. Many children will understand this intuitively, without being able to verbalize their understanding.
- Use a system. Some children begin by putting three numbers down randomly in different parts of the diagram. It is difficult to

connect them in this way, and it also is difficult to figure out exactly what went wrong. More successful solvers start in one place and work out from there.

Answer

The threes must occupy the four squares adjacent to the center. Switch any 2 for any 4.

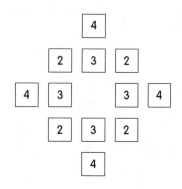

Notes

- This is a good all-group problem: Draw the diagram on tagboard and use the twos, threes, and fours from a deck of cards.
- The placement of the twos and fours is interchangeable. Any solution can be transformed into a new one simply by switching a two for a four. A few beautifully symmetric solutions are possible, and many more chaotic ones. The children probably will notice the difference.

Going Beyond

- To check childrens' ability to generalize, give them exactly the same problem again, only change the numbers to 4, 5, and 6. Some children solve it immediately and some start again from scratch.
- Play the card game Crazy Eights, with a twist. On the 4 of diamonds, for instance, instead of placing a diamond or a 4, the next player must play either a 5 or a 3 (numbers consecutive with 4; suits are ignored). It is advisable to make aces high and low, connecting them with both kings and 2s. The winner is the player to get rid of all cards first.

Patterns, Part/whole relationship

The City of Giz

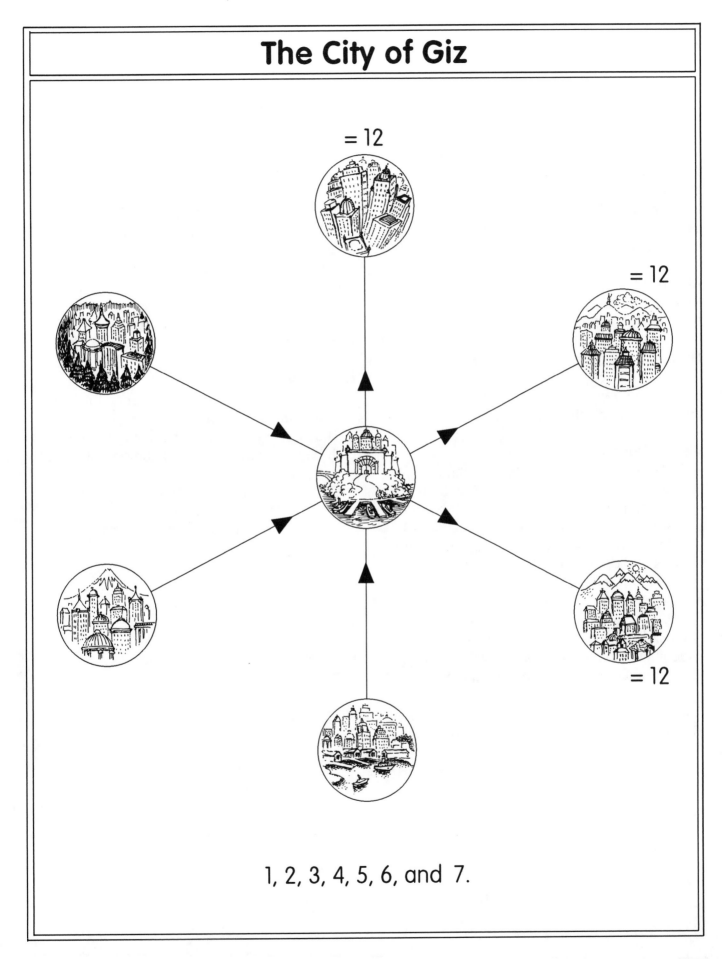

= 12

= 12

= 12

1, 2, 3, 4, 5, 6, and 7.

Directions to Children

Three magical paths run through the city of Giz, in the center of the diagram. The numbers 1 through 7 must be placed by the cities so that the numbers on any one of the three paths together add up to 12. Otherwise the magic will not last, and the city will vanish.

Materials

Pencil, the problem sheet, and small number tiles or slips of paper with the numbers on them.

Necessary Language and Concepts

Addition of three numbers; the fact that Giz is on all three paths; the location of all three paths on the grid, indicated by the arrows.

Getting Started

- Be patient. Few combinations of three numbers make 12 (7, 1, 4 and 7, 2, 3 are the only ones involving 7, for instance), but the placement of the numbers is critical. Initial failure can be looked at either as frustrating or as an opportunity to cross another wrong answer off the list.
- Figure out the significance of the city of Giz. The child who puts 7 in the center of the grid quickly realizes that no three distinct combinations make 12 and use 7. What number will work in the center and why?

Answer

The three lines must be 1 + 4 + 7; 2 + 4 + 6; 3 + 4 + 5.

Notes

- This problem has a nice symmetry to it. Again, it is one of those in which a pattern shows up unexpectedly. The middle number, 4, must go in the middle space for the problem to work. For children to see more accurately what is going on, have them list the numbers 1 through 7 and circle in red those used on one path, in green those used in the second path, and in blue those from the third path. What's the pattern? This leads nicely into an investigation of symmetry.

Going Beyond

- Try it with four paths, the numbers 1 through 9, and the target number 15. Any similarities? The next step is five paths, the numbers 1 through 11, and the target number 18. What patterns appear?
- Odd and even numbers show up in patterns here as well. What are these patterns? (This is a good opportunity to explore addition of odds and evens.)

Addition, Patterns

No More Squares

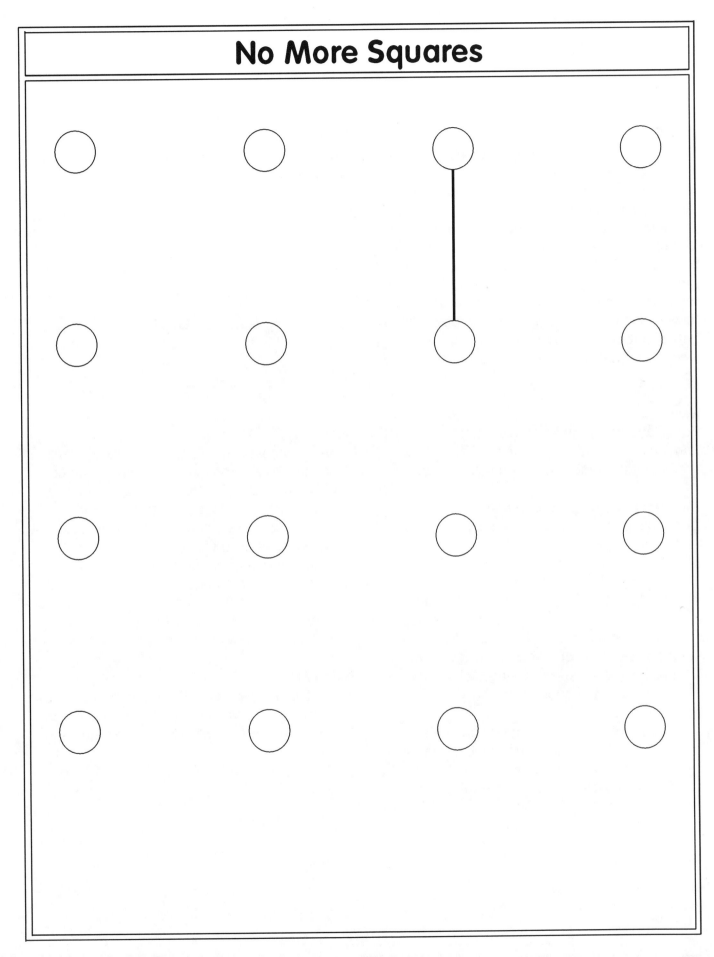

Directions to Children

Sixteen rocks are in the middle of a field. A woodcutter carrying a bundle of sticks decides to rest. He notices that his sticks fit exactly in the space between two rocks, so he puts all his sticks in the spaces. All he can see when he is done are squares—lots and lots of squares—and he is allergic to squares. So he picks up all the sticks except one and decides to put them back between the rocks so that no squares are formed. He does not put any sticks diagonally between rocks. How many sticks can the woodcutter put down without making any squares?

Materials

Pencil and the problem sheet; rods or pieces of construction paper cut to the right size. This problem can be done on a 4 x 4 geoboard.

Necessary Language and Concepts

Connecting; more and less; squares of various sizes; diagonal.

Getting Started

• Understand that squares come in more than just one size. It is possible to make squares in this problem from 4, 8, or 16 sticks. In particular, some children may forget about the 8-stick square. For younger children, it may be best to concentrate only on the 4-stick squares.
• Recognize that a small square can be filled in on three sides. There is no point in filling in just two sides of a square.
• Be willing to change an answer; the first solution is not likely to be as good as it could be if a few sticks were moved.

Answer

The maximum is 18 sticks. Here is a possible arrangement.

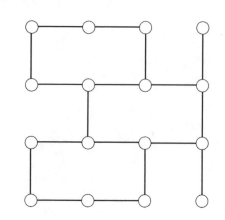

Notes

• This problem is unusual in that it asks children to avoid making something rather than to make it. This is a little difficult for some children to get used to; a few will proudly turn in a solution with every stick drawn in. Varying the assignment, though, keeps children from falling into automatic pilot. Do this in computation and other areas of math too by making sure that children see problems like: 3 + □ = 7 and □ = 3 + 4 in addition to the more common 3 + 4 = □.

Going Beyond

• Try it with a 3 x 3 or a 5 x 5 array of rocks. Are there any patterns in the the number of sticks each array will allow? Make a table and see.

Primary Colors

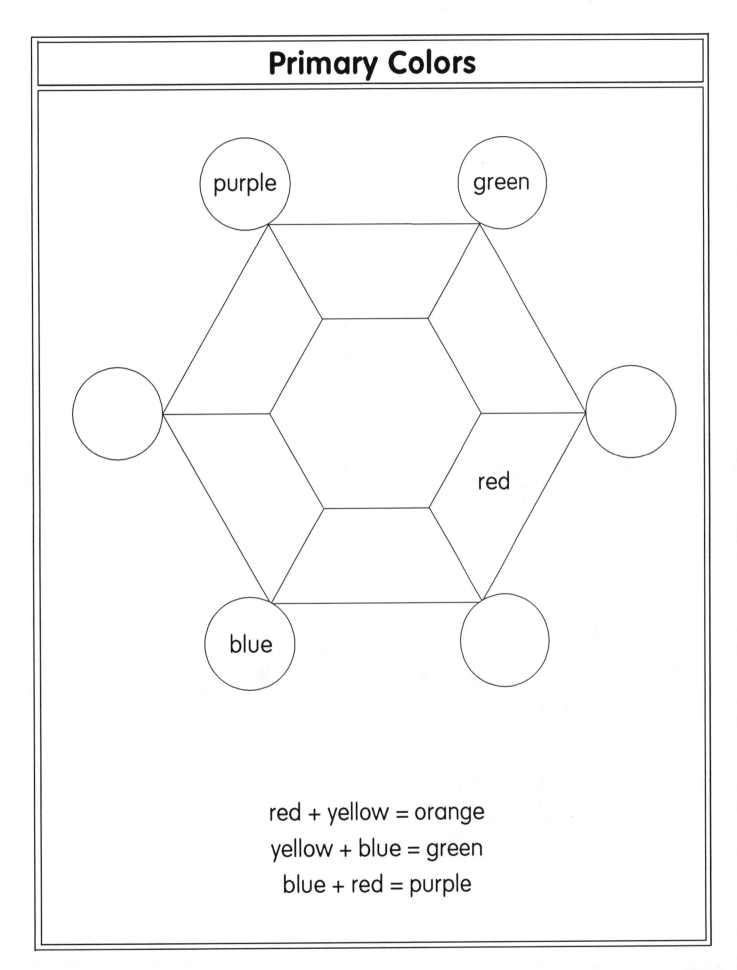

red + yellow = orange

yellow + blue = green

blue + red = purple

Directions to Children

Fill in the five spaces of the hexagon with any of the three primary paint colors (red, blue, yellow), one color to a box. The colors from any two adjacent boxes will mix together in the circle that touches them both. A yellow box next to a red box, for example, produces an orange circle. The problem gives one primary color and three of the mixtures. What colors can be placed into the remaining boxes and circles to make the whole design correct? The problem has only one answer.

Materials

Crayons or markers, the problem sheet, colored markers in the six colors.

Necessary Language and Concepts

The identification of primary paint colors and an understanding of how they are mixed to produce secondary colors; touching; circle and box or inside and outside.

Getting Started

- Start with what is known. Here are two important starting points: (1) The top box must be blue because blue is the only color contained in both purple (left circle) and green (right circle); (2) both boxes surrounding the blue circle must be blue. From there, everything falls into place. A child who starts by guessing wildly at, say, the circle at the extreme left most likely will run into a contradiction. That is frustrating, but that initial failure may lead to a more analytical way of thinking.
- Consider both the parts and the whole of the problem. Guessing the color of a circle turns out to have major repercussions all over the design, though it may seem at first like a small issue. Indeed, children who end up with a contradiction often do not notice it because they do not check whether their final color fits on both sides.

Answer

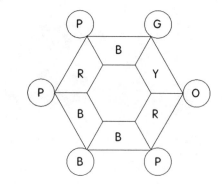

Notes

- This problem includes no numbers; it is designed to appeal to children who love art but think they do not like math. After the problem has been solved, go through the steps one at a time as a group. Children who go to pieces when asked their reasoning involving numbers often have little difficulty saying, "First, I thought about what color is part of green and purple too, and that had to be blue, so. . ."

Going Beyond

- Repeat the problem with numbers instead of colors. Add the numbers in two adjacent boxes to obtain the number in the circle. This problem is much easier, because it has multiple answers. If the two top circles are given the values 7 and 5, for instance, the box between them can have any value between 0 and 5. Despite the simplicity, less mathematical children probably will prefer the color version.

Down the Middle

Directions to Children
Cut out the shape. Then, by cutting only on the lines, divide the shape into two pieces of identical size and shape. One of the pieces may be turned over to make the pieces match.

Materials
Scissors and the problem sheet. Some children like to color their two pieces and stick them back together with tape or glue.

Necessary Language and Concepts
Apart; identical size and shape.

Getting Started
- Notice there are 12 squares altogether, and if the two pieces are to be identical sizes, each must contain 6 squares. Half the battle is solved when a child knows how many pieces must go together.
- Remember the rules. Children often forget that all cutting must be done on the lines.
- Compare pieces visually. Some children take a few minutes before starting to cut to imagine what different cuts would look like; this saves them time and energy.

Answer

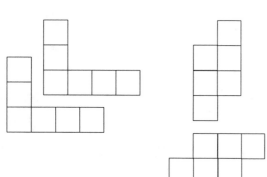

Notes
- This problem has two answers. Most children will come up with what they may call the Z shape—the leftmost three boxes combined with the top three in the next column over. Some are sure that they have found the answer. Others are concerned because the two pieces are not precisely identical unless one is turned over—mirror images.
- The other answer is much simpler, but few children will find it because an optical illusion is at work. In this solution, the leftmost three boxes are combined with the bottom row of boxes to produce an L shape. Even with the solution pointed out to them, and even after counting the boxes, some children will continue to insist that the L on the top is bigger.

Going Beyond
- Try making other patterns of 10 or 12 squares and dividing them according to the rules. Why must the patterns contain even numbers of squares?
- Could two squares be added to this diagram so that the figure could be divided along different lines?

Hit or Miss

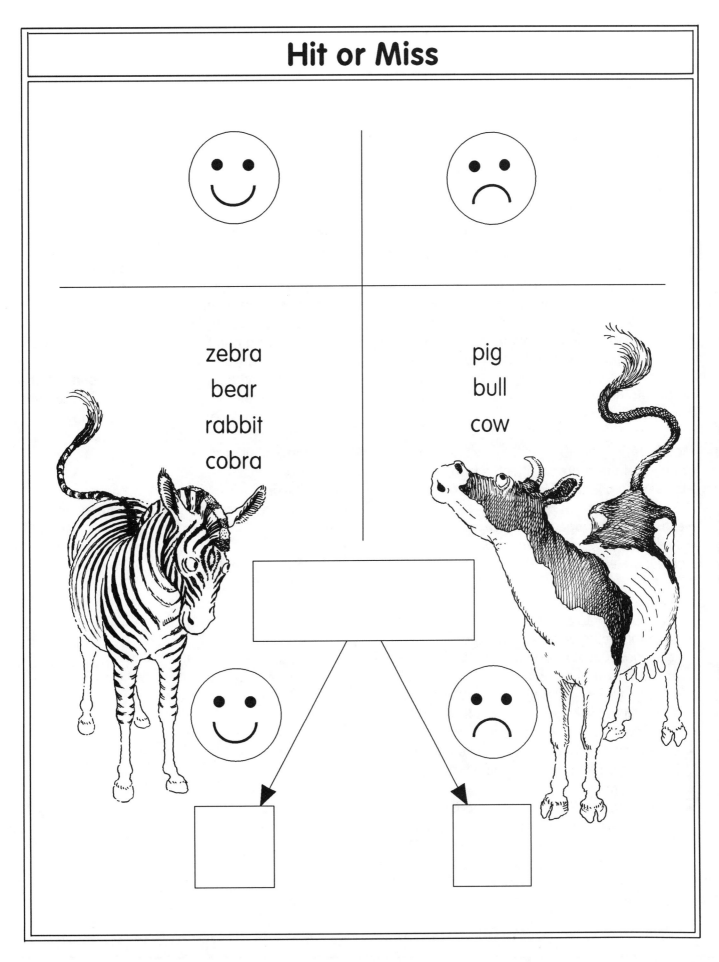

zebra
bear
rabbit
cobra

pig
bull
cow

Directions to Children

The seven names of animals are clues to finding a secret letter. The four words on the left, under the smiling face, are *hits*. They each contain the secret letter. The three words on the right, under the frown, are *misses*. They do not contain the secret letter. The problem is not to identify the letter; you do not have enough information for that yet. Instead, the problem is to find another animal name that will make the secret letter clear. That animal name is to be written in the big box. Below the animal name you select, indicate what the secret letter would be if the animal name were to belong in the hit column, and what the secret letter would be if the animal name were a miss.

Materials

Pencil and the problem sheet; a printed alphabet to check off letters is a good idea.

Necessary Language and Concepts

Hits and *misses*; words as *made up of* or *containing* letters.

Getting Started

- Pay attention to all the clues. Some children will jump to the conclusion that E is the secret letter because it appears in two *hits*—ZEBRA and BEAR—but not in any word in the *miss* column. Others will notice that B appears in every *hit* but will ignore the fact that BULL, in the *miss* column, also contains a B.
- Look for the letters that are in all the words in the hit column but none of the words in the miss column.
- Recognize that the word you choose to try must contain only one of the two possible secret letters. The words RAT or STARFISH, for instance, are of no help at all. They have to be hits because they each contain both possible secret letters.

Answer

Any word containing an R but not an A, or an A but not an R; BAT or ROOSTER would be good answers.

Notes

- Children need not be proficient readers to work this problem. In order to do well, a child need only recognize letters and know enough phonics to come up with an animal name containing a given letter. The letters lull children who don't like math into thinking that this is only a word game.
- Nearly all children automatically assume that *hits* are better than *misses*. In fact, misses are a good deal easier to deal with, as they eliminate whole groups of letters from contention all at once.

Going Beyond

- What if the word BULL had actually been a hit?
- Create your own lists of related words that contain or do not contain a letter. Create a problem for a classmate.

Castle Alert

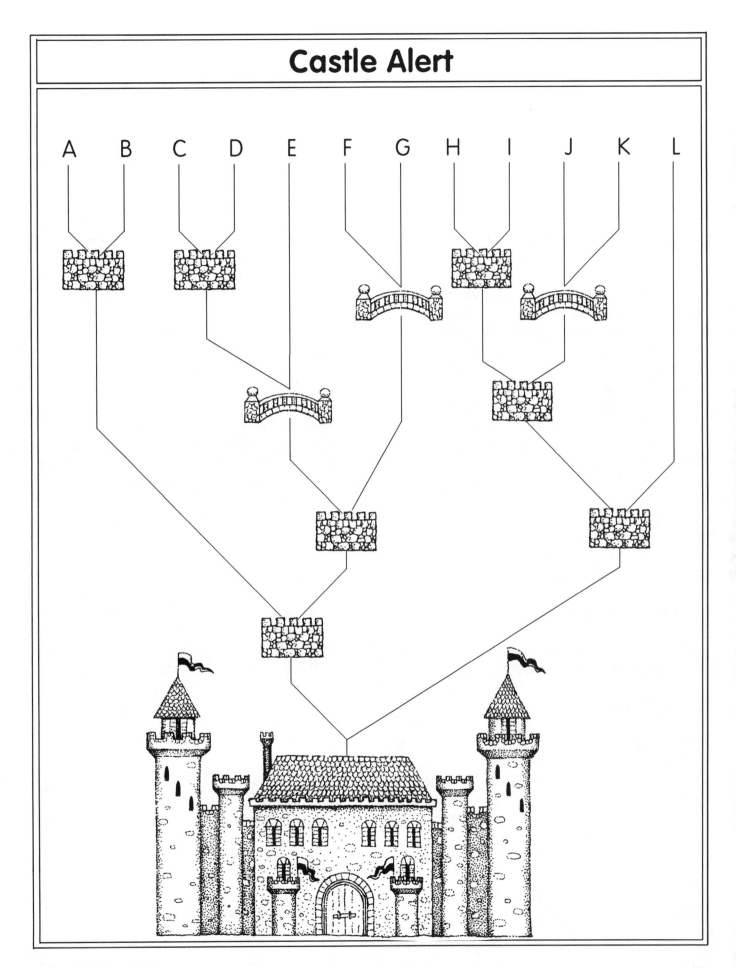

Directions to Children

The boxes marked A through L are guard boxes; each contains one guard. When an enemy army comes to invade the castle, the guards run along the paths to warn the castle. To get past a wall, two guards must be coming along each path, as the wall is too high to cross alone. Only one of the two guards actually crosses the wall and continues toward the castle; the other hoists him over and stays there. Bridges are a little different. They are designed to break in two the moment someone crosses them, leaving any other guards stranded on the other side. The royal family is interested in saving money and would prefer not to fill all the guard boxes. How few guards can they hire and still be sure that the castle will be warned in an emergency? Where should these guards be placed?

Materials

Pencil and the problem sheet. Children often like to use manipulatives like beans or white Cuisenaire® rods to represent the guards.

Necessary Language and Concepts

Thorough understanding of the way the bridges and walls work. It is useful to demonstrate for the class what happens if all 12 guard boxes are filled.

Getting Started

- Be willing to work backward. Some children, by the time they reach primary school, have realized that mazes are often much easier to solve if they go from finish to start instead of the other way around. The same is true of this problem. To get a guard over the wall in the bottom right corner, for instance, a guard must be posted at L. Working back up the walls on that side of the problem can lead quickly to a possible solution. The problem can be solved from the top down, principally

by trial and error.

- Recognize that only one person is necessary to cross a bridge and that there is no point in filling two guard boxes if they lead to the same bridge. Guards at F and G, for instance, cannot both cross the bridge below them, so only one is needed.

- Be persistent. Many children will work down to 9 or 10 guards and be satisfied. It is actually possible to lower the number down to 4.

Answer

A, B, E, F; A, B, E, G; H, I, J, L; or H, I, K, L

Notes

- This problem touches on the meanings, in formal logic, of *and* and *or*. The walls represent *and* statements; that is, both A and B must be present for a guard to continue to carry the message past the wall. The bridges represent *or* statements; either J or K must be present to carry the message past the bridge. Even six-year-olds deal with this distinction every day. Consider the frequent school phrase, "All Bluebirds with overdue library books, line up over here!" This is really two statements. In order to line up, you must be in the Bluebirds, and you must have an overdue library book. We tend to collapse these statements into one. With the help of the children, rephrase such statements into two separate statements.

Going Beyond

- Have the children make their own diagrams and give them to classmates to solve.
- How would the problem be changed if all the bridges were walls?

Building Hotels

North

West

East

South

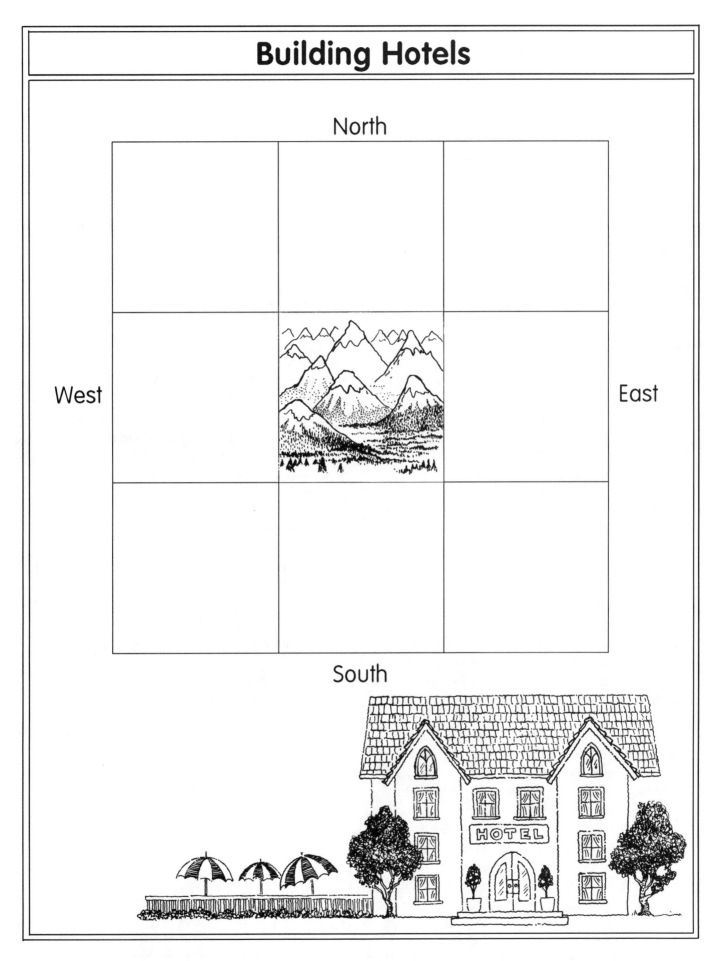

Directions to Children

This is a map of a mythical country, Squarinavia. Squarinavia is divided into nine states. The middle state is too mountainous for people to live there, but the other eight are settled. The three topmost states all qualify as *in the North*; the three on the right *in the East*; and so on. Place eight new hotels in the states so that North, South, East, and West each get four hotels.

Materials

Pencil and the problem sheet, along with 8 cubes, counters, or other small objects to represent hotels. The problem also may be worked on in a group, with squares on the floor and people representing hotels.

Necessary Language and Concepts

In the North, *in the West,* and so on. To ensure that children really understand these concepts, draw the grid on a chalkboard, and have children find states in each region before presenting the problem.

Getting Started

- Think flexibly. Some children—often those who compute quickly—will complain that the problem is impossible because you need 16 hotels to put 4 into each region and only 8 are provided. This does not invalidate the problem, but it does require those quick thinkers to stop a moment and to reflect more thoroughly: How might the problem be solvable anyway?

- Notice that the corner states are different from the others. A hotel in the lower left corner, for instance, is both in the South and in the West. A hotel in the state immediately above it, though, is only in the West. Recognizing this distinction makes finding one of the solutions much easier.

Answer

Here are two possible solutions.

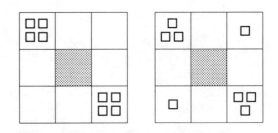

Notes

- Even children who solve the problem are surprised to see the way that 8 hotels can suddenly become 16. This is an excellent problem for destroying preconceptions about numbers: specifically, that math is full of right answers with no room for any creativity or ambiguity.

Going Beyond

- Could the problem be solved if the requirement was to have three hotels in each region? two? five? Could you get six in the West and three in each of the other regions?

- Look at a United States map. Which states are both in the North and in the West? Which in the South only? Have children shade states in according to their ideas of what regions they belong to. Be sure to introduce words like southeast.

Hop, Hop, Hop, Hop, Hop!

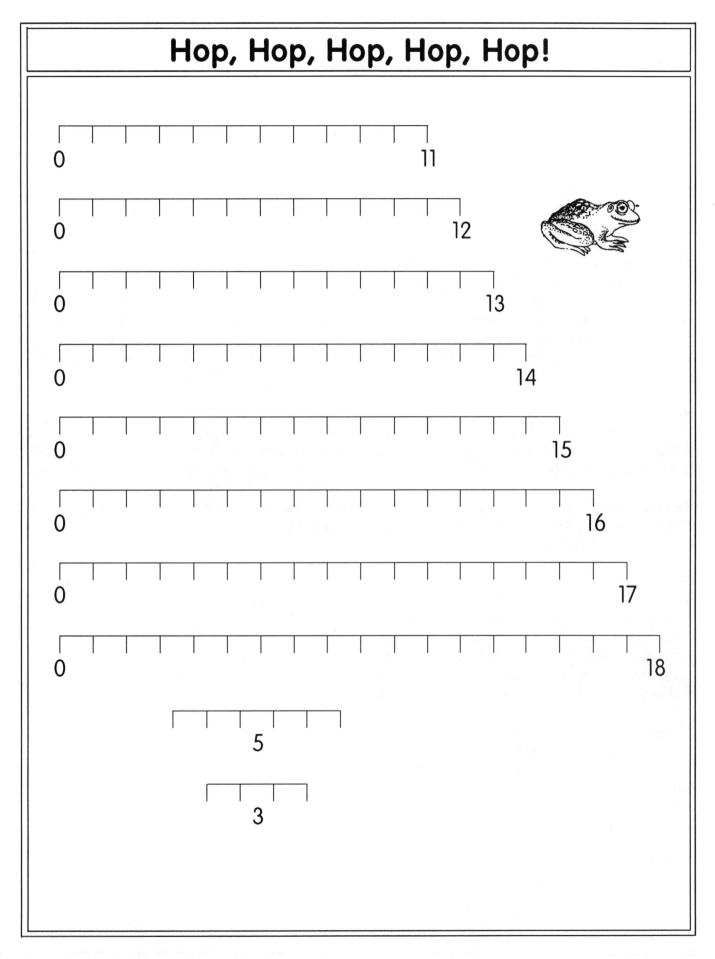

Directions to Children

A frog has friends who all live within easy hopping distance. One lives 11 units away, one 12, one 13, and so on, up to 18 units. One sunny day the frog decides to see whether she can get to each friend's door by hopping only her two favorite distances: 5 units and 3 units. What combination of three and five unit jumps will she use to get to each house? She may make these jumps in any order and may use as many of either one as she needs. How can she get to all her friends' houses? After visiting one friend, she goes back home before starting off to another friend's home.

Materials

Pencil and the problem sheet. Many children like to use the yellow and light green Cuisenaire® rods to make the problem easier to visualize.

Necessary Language and Concepts

Hops of 3 and 5 units; each of the eight problems is independent of the one before.

Getting Started

- Be willing to play with the numbers. Each can be solved, and each has several solutions, depending on what order the jumps are made. Finding an answer, though, does take a certain willingness to experiment.
- Use patterns. The solution to 11, for instance, becomes the solution to 14 just by adding on another 3, which becomes the solution to 17 just by adding three again.

Answer

$3 + 3 + 5 = 11$; $3 + 3 + 3 + 3 = 12$;
$3 + 5 + 5 = 13$; $3 + 3 + 3 + 5 = 14$;
$5 + 5 + 5 = 15$; $3 + 3 + 5 + 5 = 16$;
$3 + 3 + 3 + 3 + 5 = 17$; $3 + 5 + 5 + 5 = 18$
There are other alternatives.

Notes

- This could continue indefinitely. In fact, it is possible to make any number above 7 by using only 3s and 5s.
- The general formula, for the highest number that you cannot make by using two numbers m and n, is $(m \times n) - m - n$. In this case, that is $(5 \times 3) - 5 - 3 = 7$. There are dangers to using this formula, though. It only works when the numbers have no common factors (other than 1). Using 6 and 3, for instance, will only get the frog to multiples of 3, and using any two even numbers will only result in even numbers. It is fun to think that you can use, say, 25 and 32 to make any number greater than 743.

Going Beyond

- Try getting the frog to her friends' houses by using two different numbers.
- Make a chart showing numbers children can make using 3s and 5s and how to do it. Start with 8 and soar up toward infinity.
- Is it possible to make 7 if you allow the frog to go past her goal and then to jump backward 5 or 3 units?

Mapmaker, Color Me a Map

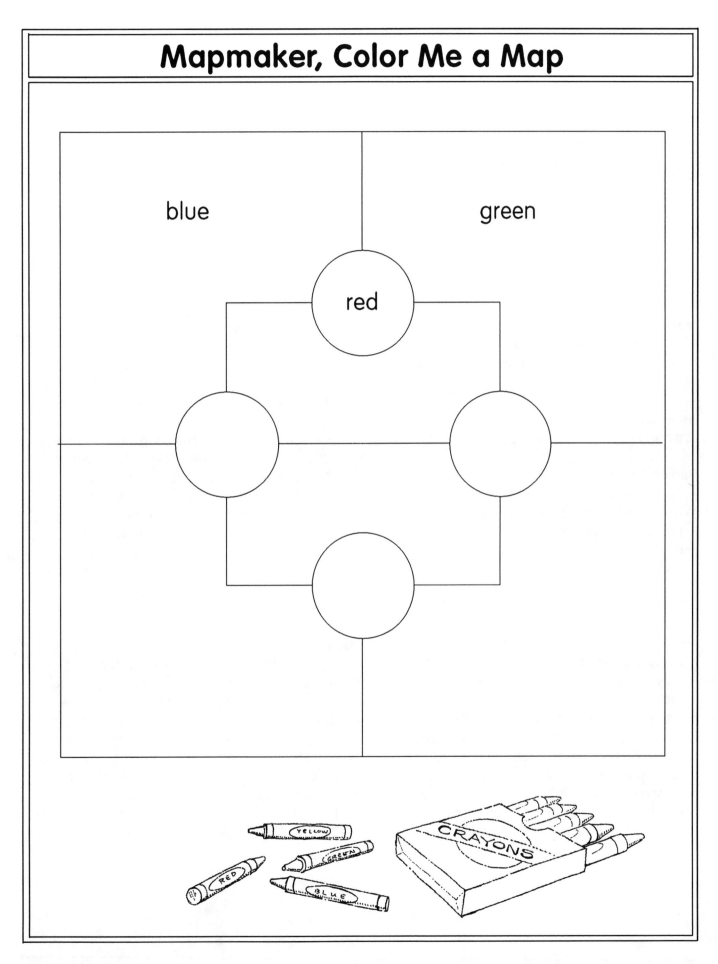

blue

green

red

Discussion for **Mapmaker, Color Me a Map**

Directions to Children

This map shows ten countries. Maps usually show adjoining countries in different colors, and this one is no different. Unfortunately, after coloring in the first three countries blue, green, and red, the mapmaker discovered that only one more color remained: yellow. How can the rest of the countries be colored so that no two that touch are the same color?

Materials

The problem sheet and four markers or crayons. Small bits of construction paper in the four colors save on mistakes.

Necessary Language and Concepts

Touching or adjoining; same and different.

Getting Started

- Take chances. Some problems in this book can be solved one logical step at a time. This one cannot. The rectangle beneath the red circle must be yellow, but the next step involves taking a chance. The remaining three circles, for instance, could be nearly any combination. As it happens, though, a few do not work out. Children who will not take a step unless they are sure often do well in some parts of math (computation in particular), but they come to a screeching halt early on in this problem.
- Use visual patterns. Both solutions have a symmetry that children see easily, especially when the regions are actually colored in (encourage careful shading so that the patterns are visible). Looking for this kind of feedback while solving the problem can really help a child make a good next guess.

Answer

The problem has four solutions, following two different principles.

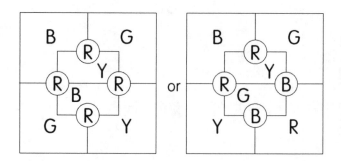

Notes

- This problem is based on a famous theory in mathematics. The four-color map theorem was for years one of math's great unresolved problems. The theorem states that no more than four colors are needed for a map, no matter how complicated the map is or how convoluted the regions. No one doubted that the theory was true, but it turned out to be remarkably hard to prove. In the end, it took the help of an enormous computer; some still hope for a simple, one-page proof to show up one of these days.

Going Beyond

- Try coloring different maps and numbers of regions. An outline map of the United States makes an interesting project, as does the map of Africa. (States that touch at one point, like Utah and New Mexico, are allowed to have the same color.) Children can make up their own maps and exchange them with classmates.
- How could this map be changed so that only three colors would be necessary?

Go for the Gold

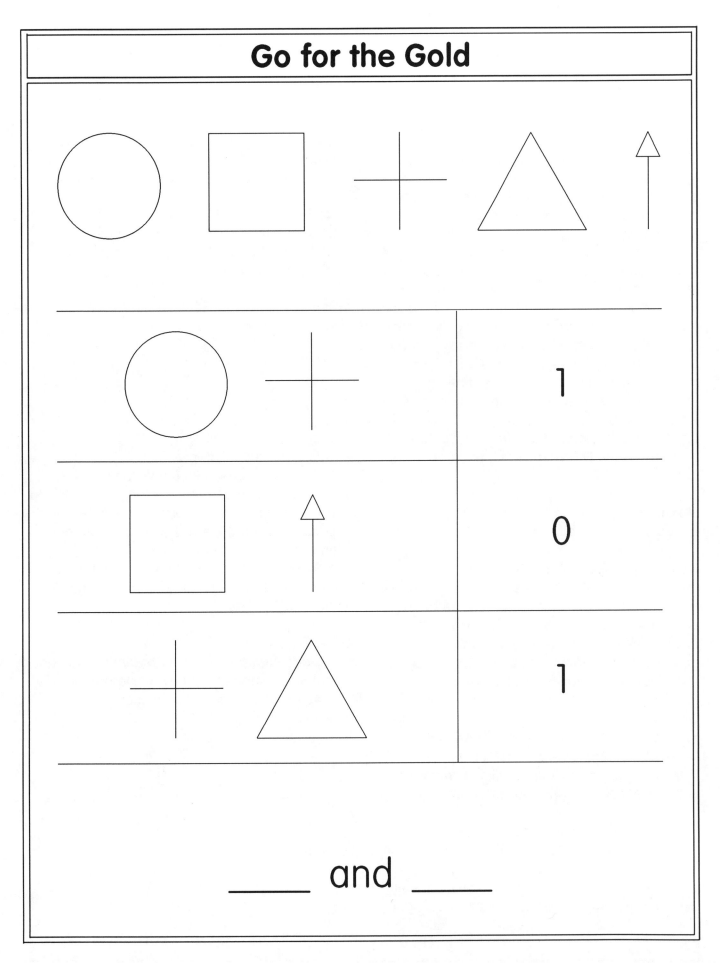

_____ and _____

Discussion for **Go for the Gold**

Directions to Children

Two of the five shapes on the top of the page are made of gold. You can put them in a gold detector to find out which two are gold. If you put two gold shapes into the detector, two lights will come on. If you put two shapes in and neither of them is gold, no lights will come on. If you put two shapes in and only one is gold, one light will come on, but it will not tell you which shape is gold. Unfortunately, the detector costs a lot of money to run. Three tries is all you can afford. But then, maybe three tries are enough. Look at the three tries pictured. One light came on when o and + were put in the detector, no lights came on when the second pair of objects were put in, and one light came on during the last try. Use the information from these three tries to find the two shapes that are made of gold.

Materials

Pencil and the problem sheet.

Necessary Language and Concepts

Identification of the five shapes and a thorough understanding of the rules. A good warm up would be picking two shapes to be gold and having children act out the machine (by beeping when lights come on or remaining silent) as you suggest possibilities.

Getting Started

- Make use of the second clue. Many children will be inclined to ignore it because the machine did not light up at all. In some ways, this is a more valuable clue than either of the others.
- Remember that two shapes are gold and that there are five altogether. At first glance, it seems clear that the + must be one of the golden shapes because it shows up in both the first and third clues when the detector showed one light.

But if the + is right, what is the other golden shape?

- Think flexibly and do not give up right away. How can the + be wrong? What other explanation could there be? Children who think creatively will think of alternatives. Children who tend to be rigid in their thinking will have a harder time.

Answer

Notes

- This is not a difficult problem, but the question of the + does throw some children off. Many of these problems are well suited to small group work; this one is particularly good for solving in pairs. Children can get emotionally attached to answers that seem to make sense, and sometimes it is helpful to have a buddy nearby who can explain where the problem lies.

Going Beyond

- Suppose that the machine had only one light that lit up whether there was one golden shape or two. Would the solution to this problem change? If so, how?

Attributes and categories, And/or

Road Map

Directions to Children

The circles represent cities. The numbers in each circle represent the number of roads going to that city. Fill in the roads on the large road map. When the roads have been drawn in, the bottom city, will have two roads from it to other cites. Roads must be more or less straight, and they may not cross each other. What will the final map look like?

Materials

Pencil, the problem sheet, and rods or toothpicks to represent roads.

Necessary Language and Concepts

Connecting; crossing; numbers representing the number of roads. Put on the blackboard a simple example map with roads and the number of roads in the circles.

Getting Started

- Discuss with your class the two completed road maps.
- Recognize that some cities give more information than others. The city in the center of the second row, for instance, could be connected almost anywhere. The cities on the edges, on the other hand, have many fewer possibilities.
- Work systematically. Careful solvers soon will find that the city in the center of the top row must be connected to each of its neighbors. That has tremendous implications for a few of the other connections, notably the cities on the extreme left and right of the diagram.
- Use diagonals. They are necessary to solve the problem.

Answer

This is the only solution.

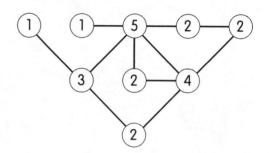

Notes

- Because each road must have a beginning and an end, the total of all the numbers in the cities must be even. It is interesting to note, however, that not all diagrams with even totals will work. In this case, for instance, the two at the extreme right can be eliminated and the problem will still work, while eliminating the two at the bottom makes the problem impossible without further changes.

Going Beyond

- Invent your own, and give them to classmates to solve. Solve them first, however, because most done at random will have no solution. It is best to draw cities and a network of roads first, then fill in the proper numbers. Then recopy the diagram without the roads.
- These can be a lot of fun things to do with childrens' own bodies. If each city is represented by a child and the roads by their own legs, arms, and heads, their contortions are amusing.

Four to Make Fifteen

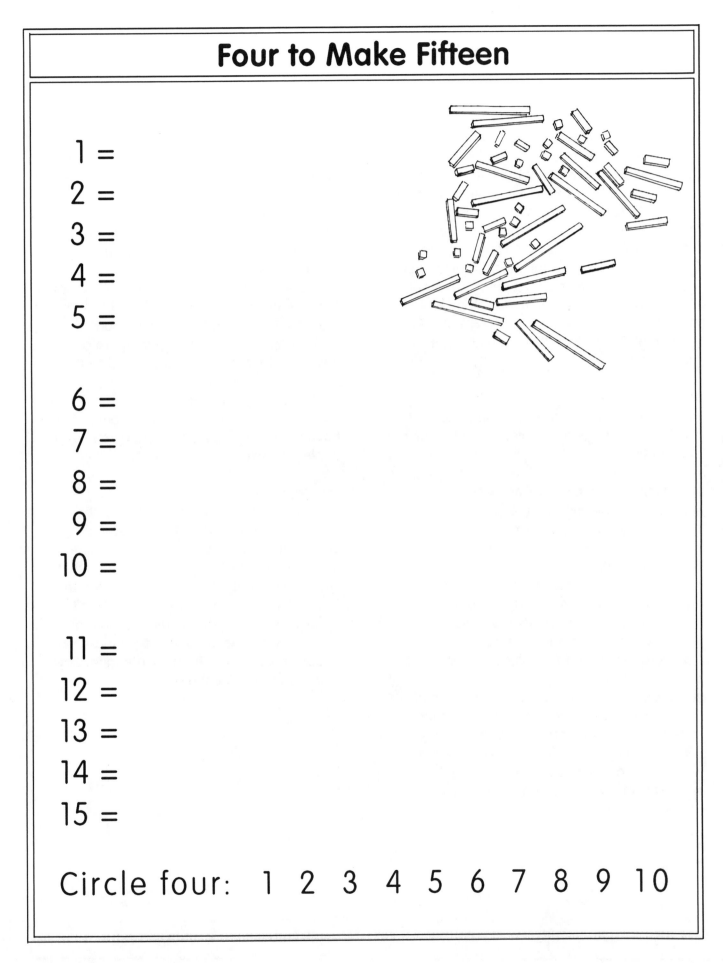

1 =

2 =

3 =

4 =

5 =

6 =

7 =

8 =

9 =

10 =

11 =

12 =

13 =

14 =

15 =

Circle four: 1   2   3   4   5   6   7   8   9   10

Directions to Children
Circle 4 numbers from the list at the bottom of the page. Use them and their sums to make as many as possible of the 15 numbers listed on the side. Circled numbers may be used alone or may be added to get new numbers. Numbers may not be used twice within the same sum. Circling 1, 7, 8, and 9, for instance, allows you to make 10 (1 + 9) or 7 (just plain 7) but not 2 (1 + 1 repeats). Write the expressions next to the number on the side, as in 10 = 1 + 9. Circle 4 different numbers and see if you can make more sums.

Materials
Pencil and the problem sheet. Cuisenaire® rods, dominoes, or other manipulatives will be helpful to children.

Necessary Language and Concepts
Addition, sums to fifteen, the idea that only circled numbers may be used.

Getting Started
- Add carefully and accurately, making sure that all possibilities have been tried.
- Choose the four numbers with care. A poor choice of starting numbers does not give the children enough possibilities, no matter how well they can add.
- Recognize the difference between choosing high and low numbers. Low numbers tend to be more valuable because adding several still produces an answer below 15. The high numbers quickly sum off the sheet.
- Be willing to change choices if they do not work out.

Answer
1, 2, 4, and 8 will give you all the numbers from 1 to 15.

Notes
- Many children will be content to turn in a sheet with 12 or 13 of the listed numbers solved. In fact, it is possible to get every one of them, and if nobody comes up with the way to do this individually, it may be worthwhile sending them back with the information that it can be done.
- The four numbers 1, 2, 4, and 8 will combine to make any number up to 15; each is double the one before it. Children can find the pattern and have fun trying to figure out why it works. Children may have less difficulty finding this solution if they work in cooperative groups. How do you make sure that you can produce 1? How about 2? If you have circled 1 and 2 already, do you need to circle 3 as well?

Going Beyond
- Give children the rods representing the numbers 1, 2, 4, and 8 and a piece of centimeter graph paper. On the first line, color 1 box gray (to stand for white). On the second line, color 2 boxes red. On the third line, color 2 red boxes and 1 gray, in either order (2 + 1 = 3). The result is a staircase with many interesting colored patterns. Children can find patterns, write them down, and read them to each other.

Addition, Patterns

Directions to Children

Divide this irregular hexagon into triangles. You may make as many straight lines as you need, but when you finish, every area inside the diagram must be a triangle. Find the fewest number of straight lines needed to form all triangles. How many triangles are formed by these lines?

Materials

Pencil, straightedge, and the problem sheet.

Necessary Language and Concepts

Triangle; dividing the shape. It can be helpful to start by drawing a square on the chalkboard and considering how to divide it into triangles.

Getting Started

• Visualize where the triangles will go before drawing them in. Some children start by drawing two or three lines that on closer inspection turn out not to have added any new triangles to the figure at all.

• Understand that it is not necessary to draw two new lines to form a triangle.

• Recognize the value of corners in the diagram. Forming a triangle by drawing a line from one corner to another has the effect of simplifying the problem. (Now we are trying to reduce a five-sided figure to triangles.) Forming a triangle by drawing a line from the middle of one side to another actually complicates things. (Now we are trying to reduce a seven-sided figure to triangles.) The quickest solution involves drawing lines only to and from the corners of the figure.

Answer

The minimum number of lines is three resulting in four triangles.

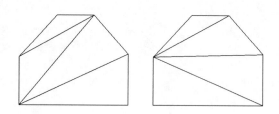

Notes

• It is possible to reduce any polygon (a closed figure with straight sides) to triangles. To find how many lines it will take, count up the sides of the polygon and subtract three. On a rainy day, it might be fun to construct a 100-sided figure and to divide it into triangles using precisely 97 straight lines.

Going Beyond

• Try the same problem with figures of different numbers of sides. Make a chart that lists the number of sides in the polygon and the number of straight lines needed to divide it into the minimum number of triangles. Look for a pattern in the chart.

• Try dividing the figure into four-sided figures, quadrilaterals. (These will not necessarily be squares or rectangles.) How many lines are necessary? When can a polygon be divided into quadrilaterals? One line will divide the hexagon into two quadrilaterals. Can a seven sided figure be divided into quadrilaterals? Can an octagon?

Mountain Squares

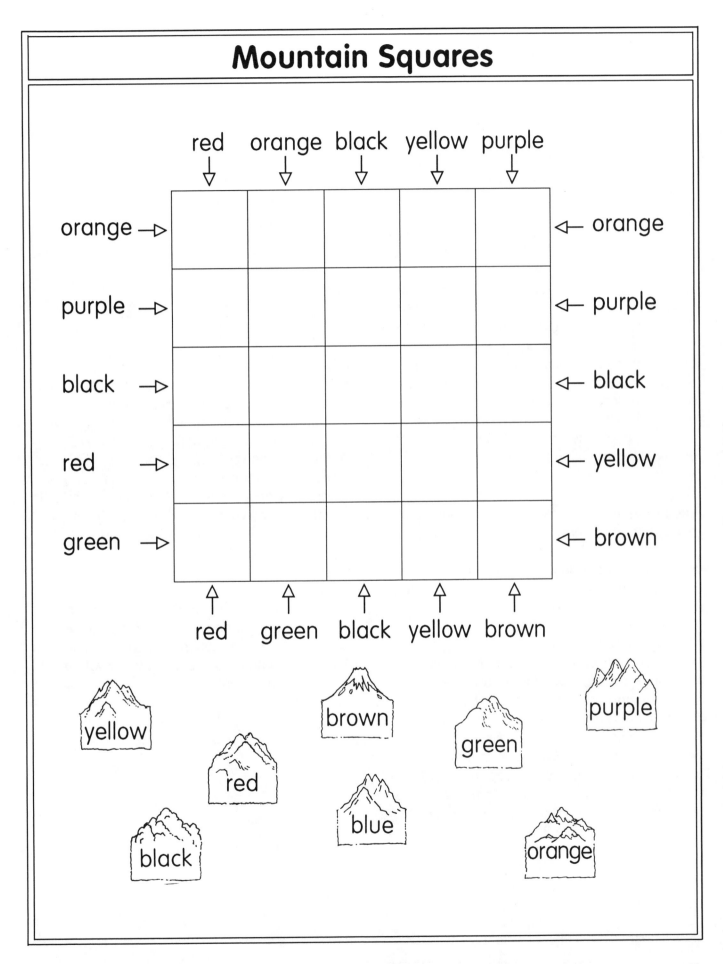

red   orange   black   yellow   purple

orange →

purple →

black →

red →

green →

← orange

← purple

← black

← yellow

← brown

red   green   black   yellow   brown

yellow

red

black

brown

blue

green

purple

orange

Directions to Children

Eight of these squares have a very tall mountain. Each mountain is a different color; the colors are circled at the bottom of the page. The other 17 squares are perfectly flat. You want to know where the mountains are, but you do not dare go into the squares because the soil will turn you to dust. So instead, stand on the edge and look. The left side of the top row has the word orange; this means that if you look across the top row, you will see an orange mountain. Other mountains might be behind it, but none is in front. The right column at the bottom says brown; going up along that column, the first mountain you see is brown. Imagine looking in from each side of each row and each end of each column and seeing the color mountain listed there. Where are all eight mountains?

Materials

The problem sheet, markers or crayons, pieces of paper in the eight colors.

Necessary Language and Concepts

Top, bottom, right, left, first; rows and columns; along the line.

Getting Started

- Use clues from all four sides of the diagram. Orange appears on the top row and also in the second column; children who pay attention to both clues have no difficulty locating the orange mountain.
- Think about the flat squares and their meaning. Because black appears on all four sides of the diagram, for instance, a careful solver not only will know where black must be but also will realize that no other mountains can be in its row or column.
- Resolve the problem caused by the blue mountain, which is not listed on the outside but must be placed somewhere anyway.

Answer

	O			
				P
		BLK		
R	B		Y	
	G			BR

Notes

- This problem typically is solved by careful reasoning; it is a problem that rewards children who think slowly and logically more than those who are willing to try many different answers. Unlike some of the similar problems in this book, however, this one does not have an obvious starting point or order in which the colors have to appear. Except for blue, each mountain may be found independently of the others.

Going Beyond

- Place your own mountains on a 5 x 5 grid, figure out what each observer would see. Write in the information. Recopy the grid with the mountains removed and trade with a classmate to solve.

Hopscotch

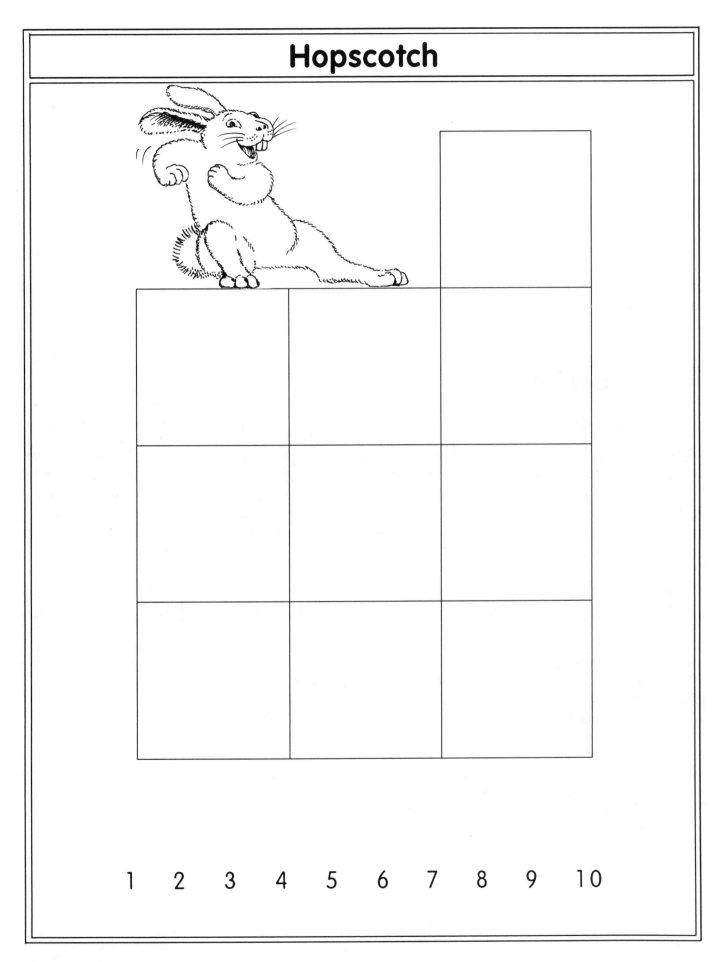

1 2 3 4 5 6 7 8 9 10

75

Directions to Children

Place the numbers 1 through 10 into the 10 boxes of the diagram so that numbers that come before or after each other are not in boxes that touch vertically, horizontally, or diagonally. The number 5, for example, may not be next to either 4 or 6.

Materials

The problem sheet and a pencil. Number tiles or small pieces of tagboard with the numerals written on them will save erasures.

Necessary Language and Concepts

Next to; diagonally, vertically, horizontally; numbers that come before or after each other.

Getting Started

- Think logically. Although the problem may be solved correctly in several hundred ways, incorrect ways number over 3.5 million. Consequently, solving the problem by trial and error is unlikely indeed.
- The keys to this problem are the center square and the square at the top right. In every solution, the center square contains either 1 or 10. Solvers are likely to have a dim idea that this must be so, though few will be able to articulate it as a general rule. Children having difficulty with the problem often come through when asked to start afresh with the number 5 in the center; this impossible task alerts them to thinking about what numbers can fit into the center box.
- Double-check after solving to make sure all the rules are followed; in particular, remember to check the diagonals for consecutive numbers.
- For younger children the diagonal rule may be dropped.

Answer

Two possibilities:

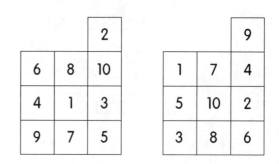

Notes

- A whole-class discussion can be tremendously useful after many children have solved the problem. Some patterns show up in all the possible solutions. The center square's significance, for example, is much more obvious to a child looking at several different solutions than to a child who has found one answer and leaves it at that.
- This problem lends itself especially well to work over a period of days. Sometimes a pattern of work-reflection-work is more effective in problem solving than one closed-end session. Children baffled on their first try often find fresh insight the next day.

Going Beyond

- Remove the upper right square, and try placing the numbers 1 to 9 among the remaining 9 squares. Why is it impossible?

The Mysterious Message

A, B, E, H, L, M, O, T, W, Y

Directions to Children

A queen used disappearing ink to write a secret message explaining where she keeps the royal treasure. To further disguise the message she used no spaces between the words . Unfortunately, she now has forgotten where the treasure is hidden. Luckily before the ink vanished, the queen took a few photographs of the message. Just in case the pictures should fall into the wrong hands, she photographed groups of only three letters at a time. Some of the letters in the message might appear twice in the photographs and some may not appear at all. The ten letters at the bottom of the page are the ten letters in the message. The shaded areas are the beginning and the end of the message. Help her figure out what the message said.

Materials

Pencil, scissors, and the problem sheet. Children may use letter tiles or cut out the 5 clues.

Necessary Language and Concepts

Beginning, middle, and end; the idea that the message is going to be reconstructed and therefore must agree with all five photographs.

Getting Started

- Proceed carefully and without jumping to conclusions. In particular, start with the photographs that mark the beginning and ending of the message.
- Recognize that the letters appearing twice within the photographs nevertheless are used only once in the message.
- Resolve the problem caused by the letter L, which is one of the ten letters listed but does not appear in any of the pictures.

Answer

BELOWMYHAT

Notes

- The fact that this problem includes no numbers obscures the amount of logic necessary to solve it. This problem is designed to encourage children to work carefully and logically. Every clue is linked tightly to the one before. Children who start more or less randomly—placing the photograph of "OWM" in the first three empty boxes, for instance—quickly run into contradictions. Starting from the outside and working in and building on the piece before yields the only solution before long.
- It is possible, but unlikely, that a child will solve the message by using the words and letters. It should be noted that no spaces occur between the words.

Going Beyond

- Write your own messages, "photograph" various pieces, and give the problems to classmates to solve. Have you provided enough information?

Logic, Systematic thought

Mayan Numbers

7

28

10

76

19

?

? 37

Directions to Children
The five examples at the top of the page show the Mayan Indian way of writing the numbers 7, 28, 10, 76, and 19. Decode the next example, and then write the number 37, using Mayan symbols.

Materials
Pencil and the problem sheet.

Necessary Language and Concepts
Decode, recognition of numbers through 99 in our system. Some familiarity with sums is helpful.

Getting Started
- Recognize that the symbols are not arbitrary but have a particular meaning.
- Be flexible. Most children, especially those who have encountered the Egyptian number problem in this book, assume that the Mayans also used a base 10 system. They did not. Good solvers quickly realize that numbers besides 10s and 100s are necessary.

Notes
- This is not precisely the Mayan number system; they had a more sophisticated way of writing numbers as large as 76, but that sophistication makes it too complicated for most second or third graders.
- The system is based on 5s and 20s. Some languages actually use the word hand to represent 5, two hands to represent 10, two hands and a foot for 15, and a person for 20; you can see where this system comes from. Children like to think about the human representation. How much is "a hand and four fingers?" How about "three people, two hands, and a foot?" How about "a hand of people"?

Going Beyond
- Discuss the advantages and disadvantages of this system.

Answer

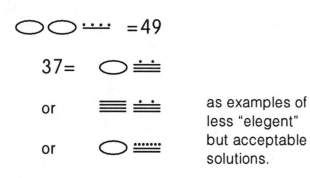

as examples of less "elegent" but acceptable solutions.